ACCENT
Your GARDEN

fine
Gardening Design Guides™

ACCENT
Your GARDEN

Creative Ideas *from* America's Best Gardeners

The Taunton Press

Special thanks to the editors, art directors, copy editors, and other staff members of Fine Gardening *who contributed to the development of the articles in this book.*

Other books in the series include: *Creating Beds and Borders, Designing with Plants, Exploring Garden Style, Gardening in Containers,* and *Landscaping Your Home.*

The Taunton Press
Inspiration for hands-on living™

The Taunton Press, Inc., 63 South Main Street, PO Box 5506, Newtown, CT 06470-5506
e-mail: tp@taunton.com

Distributed by Publishers Group West

Fine Gardening Design Guides™ is a trademark of The Taunton Press, Inc.,
registered in the U.S. Patent and Trademark Office.

COVER AND INTERIOR DESIGNER: Lori Wendin

LAYOUT ARTIST: Susan Fazekas

FRONT COVER PHOTOGRAPHERS: © LeeAnne White (large); Steve Silk © The Taunton Press, Inc. (inset)

BACK COVER PHOTOGRAPHERS: Todd Meier, © The Taunton Press, Inc. (large); Steve Silk, © The Taunton Press, Inc. (top row, left); © Suzanne Hodges (top row, center); © Lee Anne White (top row, right); Steve Silk, © The Taunton Press, Inc. (bottom row, left); © Peggy Beasley (bottom row, center); © Daniel Knight (bottom row, right)

LIBRARY OF CONGRESS CATALOGING-IN-PUBLICATION DATA
Accent your garden : creative ideas from America's best gardeners.
    p. cm.—(Fine gardening design guides)
  ISBN 1-56158-556-4
  1. Garden ornaments and furniture. I. Taunton Press. II. Fine gardening. III. Series.
SB473.5.A33 2002
  717–dc21   2001041707

Printed in the United States of America
10 9 8 7 6 5 4 3 2 1

At its best, a garden is never just a collection of beautiful plants. It is an open structure, with man-made elements that give the garden definition, individuality, and something approaching permanence.

—Michael Weishan,
The New Traditional Garden

Contents

Introduction

It's ironic that often the most important aspect of a garden isn't the plants, but rather an architectural or ornamental feature that transfigures a garden from a group of plants to a personal statement about the gardener. These accents can be something as small as a stepping stone imprinted with your dog's paw print placed among other stepping stones. Or it can be a fence, erected for privacy, that serves as the ideal backdrop for vines and other plants.

Accents can be utilitarian, such as a pathway that allows you to travel through the garden or a bench on which to rest, or they can be merely decorative, such as a piece of statuary tucked among a bed of lady's mantle.

Accents enhance the garden experience. Trellises, arbors, posts, and fences provide a structure on which to grow a gorgeous climbing rose. Birdhouses invite wildlife into the garden by giving them a place to live. Fountains and pools bring the soothing sound of moving water into the garden. Often these features are overlooked or not used to their best advantage.

In *Accent Your Garden*, we've gathered advice and ideas from some of America's best gardeners to help guide and encourage you in using a variety of features in the landscape. They take the mystery out of designing a series of pathways through your garden, selecting plants suited to a trellis, building an arbor, or bringing a sense of whimsy into the garden. They'll inspire you and give you the confidence you need to accent your own garden with features that reflect your own sense of style.

WALLS and FENCES

1

WALLS AND FENCES ARE IMPORTANT elements in the garden. They can create privacy and a sense of enclosure. They can also define the boundaries of a garden, even inviting visitors to pause and enjoy them—such as in a formal herb garden surrounded by a low-growing hedge or a picket fence with a climbing rose draped along its spine.

Designing a garden with walls and fences requires a little forethought, but with a few guidelines, you'll learn how to effectively marry these architectural features. You'll also learn to wed them with plants. Walls and fences make terrific backdrops and supports for plants; in return, plants soften their hard edges.

LEE ANNE WHITE

is a consulting editor and former chief editor of *Fine Gardening*, a Master Gardener, and a professional garden photographer.

Fences, Walls, and Hedges

Enclose *a* Garden

The stone wall enclosing this garden provides a sense of intimacy as well as a backdrop for container plantings and specimens that grow within the wall itself.

BEFORE AMERICANS EMBRACED the concept of an open, manicured lawn, our country, like many in Europe, was filled with wonderful enclosed gardens. Just take a leisurely walk through one of our historic districts. The old homes of Savannah, Charleston, Key West, Santa Fe, New England, and many early American towns are filled with lush walled gardens and cozy cottage gardens. Gardens that make you want to stop and chat over the fence, or strain to peer over a high wall or through a hedge to see what's on the other side.

Even if they're primarily relegated to backyards, we can still enjoy the warmth and intimacy of an enclosed garden. In our fast-paced world, we need a quiet place to relax more than ever before.

Enclosures—whether created from walls, fences, or hedges—form an architectural backbone for the garden.

In addition to privacy, this solid fence serves as a backdrop, highlighting the variety of textures, shapes, and colors in the garden.

They define boundaries and divide large areas into smaller, more manageable spaces. In small gardens, dividing the space into multiple "rooms" often makes them seem larger. Walls, fences, and hedges can screen unwanted views and provide vines a support upon which to scamper, while adding a vertical accent to the garden. Properly placed, they even protect plants from harsh winds, change the patterns of sunlight and shade in a garden, and provide a solid backdrop for colorful plantings.

DESIGN ENCLOSURES WITH INDIGENOUS MATERIALS

When it comes to designing an enclosure, the possibilities are endless. In fences, you'll find painted pickets, rustic split rails, solid cedar planks, woven wattle, wrought iron, Asian-inspired bamboo, and others. Walls, whether high or low, can be constructed from stone, brick, stucco, or manufactured materials. Hedges may be formal or informal, evergreen or deciduous, and created from shrubs or trees.

Choose a style that blends with the architecture of your home and that reflects the indigenous materials of your region. In New England, stacked stone is a natural. If you live in a cottage, a white picket fence could be perfect. And in the sun-baked Southwest, adobe walls are always appropriate. Yet, don't limit yourself to a single selection. Mixing materials helps define different garden spaces, or rooms.

For privacy, use taller fences, walls, and evergreen hedges that create solid screens. For a more neighborly atmosphere or to preserve a view, a low stone wall, loosely planted hedge, or low fence with widely spaced pickets opens matters up considerably. Place colorful and fragrant flower beds around your fence and you've issued an open invitation to neighbors for a friendly morning chat.

ACCENT WALLS AND HEDGES WITH PLANTS

Of course, enclosures don't guarantee a sense of intimacy. A small area surrounded by a tall, bare wall can feel like a prison cell. One way to accent bare walls and fences is with attractive container plantings. The containers, as well as the plants, should contrast with the color and texture of the wall or fence. Garden benches and other outdoor furniture can also dress up a wall.

To create a truly romantic garden, cover your wall with climbing plants like English ivy (*Hedera helix*), clematis, hyacinth bean (*Dolichos lablab*), or climbing roses for an old, established look. Vines with rootlets will attach themselves to just about any surface, but if you want to grow a twining vine or one

A brick wall adds a sense of formality to this southern garden.

A tall, solid screen provides privacy.

Container plantings provide a colorful contrast to a bare wooden fence.

A gate draws the eye to the garden beyond the enclosed garden.

Bricks delineate formal garden from casual woodland garden beyond.

with tendrils, you'll need to install a trellis against the wall or fence.

As an alternative to climbers, try espaliering a fruit tree, firethorn (*Pyracantha coccinea*), quince (*Chaenomeles* spp.), or *Camellia*. You'll be delighted with their flowers, fruit, fall foliage, or year-round greenery, depending on which plant you choose.

Small-leaved evergreens like boxwood (*Buxus* spp.), yew (*Taxus* spp.), and holly (*Ilex* spp.) are popular for formal hedges. They are

most often planted in straight lines or geometric patterns and pruned frequently during the growing season. Sometimes, small-leaved deciduous shrubs like privet (*Ligustrum* spp.) are also clipped into formal hedges, but most deciduous shrubs—from *Forsythia* and burning bush (*Euonymus alatus*) to Vanhoutte spirea (*Spiraea × vanhouttei*) and lilacs (*Syringa* spp.)—are usually planted in a staggered fashion and allowed to grow freely into informal hedges which are

pruned less frequently. I even visited a garden recently where beech trees (*Fagus* spp.) were being pleached into a hedge.

As you plan your garden enclosure, keep in mind that in most cases your wall, fence, or hedge should serve as a backdrop for plantings rather than as a focal point. Of course, that doesn't mean that it can't be attractive. After all, I prefer a mossy brick wall over plain chain link any day.

Boxwood, yew, and holly all work well as formal hedges but require frequent pruning.

"Enclosures—whether created from walls, fences, or hedges—form an architectural backbone for the garden."

S. ANDREW SCHULMAN

is a Seattle-based land-scape designer, garden writer, and photographer. He lectures frequently on rose gardening and garden design.

The Irresistible Appeal of Pickets

Pickets and perennials are a perfect pair. Fences are ideal back-drops for many plants.

NEIGHBORS CHAT OVER THEM on a Sunday afternoon. Smoke from the barbecue drifts through them on the Fourth of July. Little boys on bicycles clatter sticks along their flanks as they streak by. We may take them for granted as emblems of domestic comfort, but picket fences are more than just a suburban cliché. They're a classic American landscape feature—as indispensable as pumpkin pie at Thanksgiving or hot dogs at a baseball game. They also happen to be some of the most versatile and adaptable structures in the garden design repertoire.

Although it's one of our favorite garden structures, the picket fence is not an American invention. Picket fences appear in Chinese paintings from the eighth century, and were common European garden fixtures as early as the 14th century. Picket fences arrived in North America with the very first settlers. The pilgrims at the Plymouth colony used them to dress up gardens and contain livestock, and by 1705, colonial Williamsburg passed an edict that all houses along Duke of Gloucester Street were to be enclosed by walls, pales (pickets), or post-and-rail fences within six months of their construction. By the time the United States declared its independence, the picket fence, often as not painted white, had become a favorite garden enclosure.

ENCLOSE A YARD AND GARDEN ATTRACTIVELY AND EASILY

My wife and I always say we owe our picket fence to the dog. The fine print on our pure-bred puppy's purchase contract required an enclosed yard. Enclosed, that is, with a fence at least 5 feet tall. The breeder wasn't kidding—she wanted photographic evidence before she would hand over the dog!

We had three weeks to erect a fence on a site with some serious design challenges. Our yard occupies the entire end of a city block, with 200 feet of road frontage on two well-traveled urban streets. Since the yard sits above street level atop a 4-foot-tall retaining wall, our fence would also tower at least 9 feet above the sidewalk.

We needed a fence that could contain a large dog without turning our yard into a fortress. It would have to be quick to install, attractive, and blend with our home's neo-colonial architecture. Although I'd long thought of them as hopelessly banal and

hokey, we both realized that a picket fence would satisfy our needs. With some prodding, necessity overcame my prejudice, the picket fence went up, and the puppy arrived on schedule.

After living with our fence for several years, I've recognized its many advantages. Ease of construction is certainly one of the picket fence's greatest assets. British gardeners may sneer at our fences as flimsy and insist upon walls of brick and stone, with their enduring solidity. But for ever-mobile Americans, who average a move every five or six years and are accustomed to a cheap supply of lumber, the picket fence holds an irresistible appeal.

The earliest picket fences were little more than sharpened sticks, or palings, driven into the ground. The usual modern configuration, with posts and rails to support the palings, is a later refinement. It simplifies installation, provides greater structural integrity, and extends the life of the palings by keeping them out of contact with the soil.

To add strength and prevent rot in Seattle's notoriously soggy winters, the posts supporting our fence are not set directly into

Picket fences are a classic American landscape feature. For design use, they are both practical and adaptable for creating a sense of enclosure.

Its virtues merit its popularity. Light and airy picket fences are right at home in the most casual of ornamental gardens.

the ground. Instead, they are nested onto steel pipes set into concrete footings. Our entire fence took all of two working days to install. The only difficult part was the painting, which we did ourselves. So far, the fence has withstood two record-breaking windstorms and the constant onslaught of our 80-pound Akita. When the time comes to repaint, maybe we'll manage Tom Sawyer's gambit and con the neighbors into doing it for us.

POSTS AND PALINGS DETERMINE CHARACTER

Speed and ease of installation are only the first of the picket fence's many virtues. As a true convert, I've grown to appreciate its considerable ornamental value. The pointed pal-

ings that make up the traditional picket fence probably began as a deterrent against livestock, wild animals, and trespassers. Over time they evolved to include a range of elaborate and fanciful patterns. The tips can be rounded or pointed, concave or convex, symmetrical or asymmetrical—any pattern that the carpenter can manage.

Ornament needn't be limited to the tips of the palings either. The vertical edges can be carved into any imaginable silhouette: Queen Anne chair backs, fleur-de-lis, even birds. Elaborate patterns of solid and empty spaces can play themselves out along the length of the fence.

The general character of any picket fence is largely determined by the width and spacing of the posts and palings. The palings can vary from extremely narrow to wide and flat. Where privacy is an issue, broad palings can be set closely. We chose narrow, closely spaced palings for our fence, so it appears relatively light and airy from the sidewalk, despite its great height.

If you want your fence to appear longer, select posts that approximate the palings in size and shape. Posts that contrast with the palings, either in weight, height, or both, punctuate the fence and reduce its apparent length. Our fence posts are tall and heavy, with turned finials at their tops. They break up the fence's long horizontal run and establish a lively visual rhythm along the street. This kind of visual rhythm accounts for much of the picket fence's appeal in the landscape. Think how hard it is to resist rapping those pickets when you walk past them!

HANDSOME SUPPORTS FOR OLD-FASHIONED CLIMBERS

Because picket fences allow light and air to circulate freely, they make ideal supports for climbing plants of all kinds. I like to drape my own with old-fashioned roses and clematis. These long-blooming plants echo the fence's traditional style and also tolerate the occasional hard pruning required when it's time to repaint the fence.

Annual climbers are also easy to work around when a picket fence needs periodic maintenance. Old-fashioned annual climbers such as sweet peas (*Lathyrus odoratus*) and morning glories (*Ipomoea* spp.) are especially appropriate. Hyacinth bean (*Lablab purpureus*) and blue cup-and-saucer vine (*Cobaea scandens*) make lovely cool accents on a white picket fence. Scarlet runner beans (*Phaseolus coccineus*), cardinal climber (*Ipomoea* × *multifida*), and the firecracker blooms of Spanish flag (*Ipomoea lobata*) make

for dazzling contrast. All look wonderful dangling among the palings. Avoid covering your fence with ivy, Virginia creeper (*Parthenocissus quinquefolia*), or any other climber that adheres by holdfasts. These plants can damage the finish on your fence and diminish its life span.

A picket fence makes an ideal backdrop for borders of perennials and flowering shrubs. The vertical thrust of the palings and posts are an outstanding formal accent for naturally bushy, mounded, or arching plants

Paling height and width determine character. Tall, broad palings create privacy while narrow, widely spaced palings are less substantial.

"Ease of construction is certainly one of the picket fence's greatest assets."

Picket fences provide the ideal support for climbing plants. Vertical palings perfectly accent trailing plants such as shrub roses.

such as shrub roses, peonies, or asters. A white picket fence also lends a special brand of visual lift and sparkle to dark, heavy-textured, broad-leaved evergreens. Plantings need not be overly elaborate. A simple line of tufted blue fescue (*Festuca glauca*) or evenly spaced clumps of lavender (*Lavandula* spp.) makes an effective foil to any picket fence.

LEAVE A LITTLE ROOM FOR PAINTING AND REPAIRS

If you plan on a wide border or a particularly long fence, consider leaving a narrow passage between the fence and the rear of the border.

This arrangement allows easier access for painting and fence repairs. If you plan to maintain a lawn on one or both sides of your picket fence, consider setting it atop a strip of gravel or crushed rock over landscape fabric. If the strip extends at least a foot or so on either side of the fence, you'll find mowing and trimming the lawn much easier.

Take it from this former skeptic—a picket fence doesn't have to be trite. If they strike you as too common, remember that their virtues merit their popularity. Easily constructed and relatively inexpensive, picket fences are at home in the most casual of gardens or in highly geometric, formal schemes. Their range of style and the ease with which they blend with traditional garden designs and architecture recommend them wherever the home landscape requires a low-cost barrier.

The design mirrors the site. The color and form of this fence reinforce the informality of its surroundings.

ANDY BEASLEY

landscapes his home in
the Colorado Rockies
with stone, brick, and
other low-maintenance
materials to accent
the natural beauty
around him.

Stacking a
Dry
Stone Wall

The irregular shapes of
fieldstones are ideal for
creating an informal
stone wall that will last
for generations.

I WAS ABOUT 7 years old when my brother and I rigged up a low-tech trolley. We strung steel cable between two trees on opposite sides of a hillside stone wall, put a pulley on the wire, and added a hay hook for a handle. Our jerry-built contraption made for quite a ride and, if we lifted up our legs at just the right moment, it would carry us over the wall and on to the downhill tree. It was exhilarating—until an unmusical twang announced the snapping of the cable. My brother was hurtling toward the wall at just that moment. He landed on his back, right on top of the heap of stones.

Luckily, he wasn't hurt, but I think my respect for the strength, solidity, and sheer immobility of stone walls took root at that very moment. Nothing matches a stone wall for a feeling of permanence, and their beauty, to me, is unsurpassed. During my youth, I developed a love for the lichen-covered stone walls that snaked across hillsides

Strength and beauty are the hallmarks of stone walls. Through changing seasons and passing years, stone walls provide an elegant accent to any landscape.

shaded by oaks and pines that weren't even seedlings when the stones were first laid.

Their strength and beauty make stone walls perfect for marking property boundaries, for landscaping, and as an elegant accent to any garden. They're also a great way to dispose of stones removed from a new garden or a cleared field. The randomly shaped fieldstones hauled from the ground are ideal for building an informal-looking structure. For a formal look, use ashlar, stone that has been cut into building-block shapes.

Freestanding stone walls are usually built using one of two basic techniques. If a completely rigid wall is the goal, you'll need a wet, or mortared, wall—one built upon a sturdy concrete foundation and with mortar between the stones. This type of wall requires a foundation dug below the frost line. Otherwise, winter's freezing and thawing may heave the earth and crack the concrete. Construction is complicated enough to warrant hiring a mason.

The other style, and my favorite, is the dry wall. It is laid up without mortar and doesn't require a rigid foundation. A freestanding, rubble-filled, dry-stone wall 3 feet or less high is easy to build, even for beginners. In fact, it's not much more complicated than putting together a jigsaw puzzle. If the wall is carefully constructed, gravity will help hold its stones in place. Anyone who can follow my simple guidelines can build a dry wall that will be admired by generations to come.

THINK LONG TERM WHEN DESIGNING A WALL

If there's one rule about stone walls, it is—as my brother learned long ago—they don't move. So design your wall with the care and foresight you would devote to any permanent structure.

If you plan to build a wall along your property line, it is essential to check a plat or site map. After you've labored to lay a magnificent wall is not the time to learn you've encroached on your neighbor's land or crossed a locally mandated setback. For a sizable wall, you may need a building permit. Walls more than 3 feet high require a permit in many parts of the country and are best left to professional masons anyway.

Once the site has been selected, use a string and stakes, or even a garden hose, to lay out the course of the wall. Don't make this step too complicated. For a straight wall, just stretch a length of string between two stakes. For a curving wall, experiment by arranging a garden hose until you have an arc that fits the site and pleases the eye.

Once you know where the wall is to go, use a pick and shovel to dig a foundation trench. For a dry wall, the foundation should be deep enough to set the bottom course, or row, of stones well into the ground. Some builders dig a foundation more than a foot

deep and line the bottom with gravel, but I've found a simple trench, 6 to 8 inches deep, to be sufficient. If you have very soft soil, you might find it best to dig your foundation down to a layer of hardpan.

Base the width of the foundation on the type of stone you're using and on the wall's eventual height. Square, flat stones lay up fairly easily, so a relatively narrow foundation, one a little wider than half the wall's height, should suffice. A 3-foot-high wall will need a foundation roughly 20 inches wide. Irregular stones require a wider foundation for good stability, so plan on a foundation just a few inches narrower than the wall's eventual height. For a wall that will rise 3 feet aboveground, make a foundation about 3 feet wide. It's important to be a little generous because a 3-foot-tall wall may well be closer to 4 feet in actual height since some of the

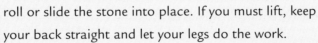

Take Simple Precautions when Working with Stones

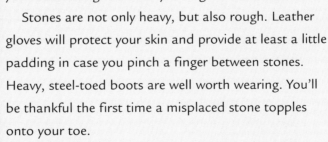

Unlike projects requiring dangerous power tools or risky procedures, building with stones is quite benign—but there are a few things to watch out for. Perhaps the biggest risk is back injury, so be careful moving large stones. Roll them into place, or use a pry bar to help position them. To move larger stones, rest one end of a stout plank about where you want the stone to go and place the other end on the ground. Using the plank as a ramp,

roll or slide the stone into place. If you must lift, keep your back straight and let your legs do the work.

Stones are not only heavy, but also rough. Leather gloves will protect your skin and provide at least a little padding in case you pinch a finger between stones. Heavy, steel-toed boots are well worth wearing. You'll be thankful the first time a misplaced stone topples onto your toe.

Finally, always wear safety glasses while working. When prying stones with a bar or when dropping a stone onto a pile of rocks, there's the chance a stone chip or piece of dirt may take wing and fly toward your eyes.

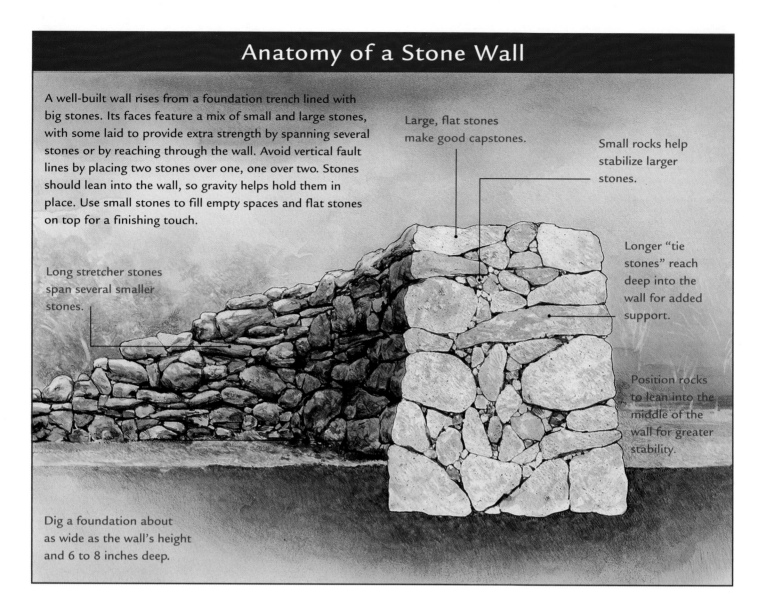

Anatomy of a Stone Wall

A well-built wall rises from a foundation trench lined with big stones. Its faces feature a mix of small and large stones, with some laid to provide extra strength by spanning several stones or by reaching through the wall. Avoid vertical fault lines by placing two stones over one, one over two. Stones should lean into the wall, so gravity helps hold them in place. Use small stones to fill empty spaces and flat stones on top for a finishing touch.

Large, flat stones make good capstones.

Small rocks help stabilize larger stones.

Longer "tie stones" reach deep into the wall for added support.

Long stretcher stones span several smaller stones.

Position rocks to lean into the middle of the wall for greater stability.

Dig a foundation about as wide as the wall's height and 6 to 8 inches deep.

stones will be underground as part of the foundation. Once the trench has been dug, level the bottom with a steel rake.

GET THE MATERIALS READY

With the foundation dug, arrange the stones for use. Make sure you have an adequate supply of accessible stones. Even small walls require a lot of stone, so don't plan to encircle your property with stone walls unless you have a lot of good stones lying around or you happen to own a quarry.

If you don't have a ready supply, visit a stone yard to select suitable building materials. To estimate how much stone you'll

need, multiply the width times the height times the length of the wall. If you're building a wall 3 feet tall, 3 feet wide, and 30 feet long, you'll need some 270 cubic feet of stone. Typically, a ton of stones—whether they are the irregular fieldstones known as rubble, or the flatter wall or flag stone—contains about 15 cubic feet of building material. To make sure you have a good selection of sizes and shapes, add another 20 percent or so to the total.

One advantage of buying stone is that you can have it delivered right to the job site instead of lugging all the stone yourself. Put aside the largest stones for the foundation, and spread the small-, medium-, and larger-sized rocks in groups according to size. The very best long or flat stones are to be used as "stretcher stones" to run across the top of a short row of smaller stones, as "tie stones" to add stability to the wall, and as "capstones," to provide a finishing touch on top. Long, flat stones are also used to make the end of a wall look pleasing. I like to think of the various piles as an artist's palette.

Traditional, rubble-filled, freestanding walls are actually composed of two parallel rows of stone, one for each face of the wall. The face stones, those on the exposed sides of the wall, should be right against the outside edge of the foundation. The space between the rows is filled with leftover rubble and small stones as construction progresses.

USE THE BIGGEST ROCKS FIRST

With the site and stones ready, it's time to build. For the foundation, roll the largest stones into the trench. Their size and weight will make the foundation strong, and it's easier to roll them into a trench than it is to position them higher in the wall. Use large, irregular stones in the trench too—it's easier to position them in the foundation than to fit them in as construction progresses.

When placing foundation stones, it's important to anchor them securely in the earth. Use a garden trowel to dig recesses for any odd projections on the stones. Try to place the foundation stones so the flattest side is up, but be sure to leave a pleasing surface on what will be the face of the wall too—big stones are likely to be taller than the foundation is deep, so they will be visible. Once the first course is laid, fill in any gaps between the stones with small rocks to help steady the foundation during the inevitable settling process. Soil left over from digging

"Nothing matches a stone wall for a feeling of permanence, and their beauty, to me, is unsurpassed."

the foundation can be used to fill in gaps along the outside edge of the wall.

For additional strength and stability, arrange the foundation stones and rubble fill in a slight V shape, with the center lower than the tops of the outside edges, like a valley. Then, later courses will have a tendency to lean into the middle of the wall and rest upon each other, thus increasing the wall's stability. Some builders taper, or "batter," the wall so that they slope inward about 1 inch for every foot of the wall's height. Gravity will help pull stones into the wall instead of nudging them out onto the ground.

As you add succeeding courses, place the face stones first, then use debris to fill in behind them. Rather than laying a course of stone the entire length of the wall and then starting with another row of stones, it's easier to concentrate on a 10- to 15-foot stretch of wall at a time. At one end of the working

Use small rocks to fill in between larger ones, even in the foundation. By eliminating empty spaces in the wall, small stones contribute to the wall's stability.

area, the wall may be nearly completed while the other end is just getting started. When you finish at one end, add foundation stones at the other.

ADD STONE WEDGES TO STABILIZE BIG ROCKS

While building, use lots of wedge-shaped pieces of stone to help stabilize larger stones on the faces of the wall. These wedges are best positioned from the inside of the wall, where other stones and the rubble fill will help hold them in place. Wedges placed from the outside of the wall may fall out, loosening the stones they were supporting.

Use smaller stones and debris to fill voids inside the wall as you build. By eliminating open spaces the larger stones could settle into, the small rocks make a vital contribution to the wall's long-term stability. Some builders say constructing a stone wall is like putting together a 3-D jigsaw puzzle. They memorize the shape of the hole they need to fill, then look for a rock that will fit. It gets easier with practice.

As the wall progresses, you may want to use a level or a length of twine strung tautly between two stakes as a guide to help keep it true, though I just do it by eye. To prevent sections of the rising wall from toppling over, periodically use a longer stone as a "tie stone," to bridge the gap in the middle of the wall. These should be laid perpendicular to the wall's faces and stretch from one outside edge to the other to help lock the two rows of stones into a cohesive whole. If you don't have stones long enough to reach across the wall, shorter ones that tie one face to the inner core will also work. Make frequent use of this technique.

PLACE ONE STONE OVER TWO, TWO OVER ONE

As the wall rises, place stones in succeeding layers over gaps in the course beneath them. The idea is to avoid large vertical fault lines that will weaken the wall. Use the old mason's rule of two over one, one over two. And be sure to use a good mix of sizes—walls built with all the same-sized stones don't look as pleasing.

Although I don't believe there's such a thing as an ugly stone wall, you should select the most attractive stones for the wall's faces.

One good side is all it takes, provided you have become adept at using wedges to secure irregularly shaped rocks.

Periodically step back to evaluate your progress. Make sure the stones look good together and that you've avoided any wall-weakening gaps or unsightly seams. When you reach the end of a section, either vertically or horizontally, draw on your pile of long and flat stones. They can be used as capstones to dress up the top of the wall and on the ends of the wall to hide the rubble that fills the wall's core.

A WALL WORTH ADMIRING

Few accomplishments provide as much satisfaction as completing a stone wall. Once you're done, you're done. Maintenance requirements are practically nil. Stone wall upkeep consists of replacing the occasional stone that topples off the wall during the winter. To me, stone walls have an enduring beauty that adds richness and texture to any landscape. I've found their appeal to be almost universal. Nearly everyone likes them—even my brother.

Use large stones on the bottom of the wall. They provide stability to the finished wall, and you won't have to struggle to lift them to a higher position in the wall.

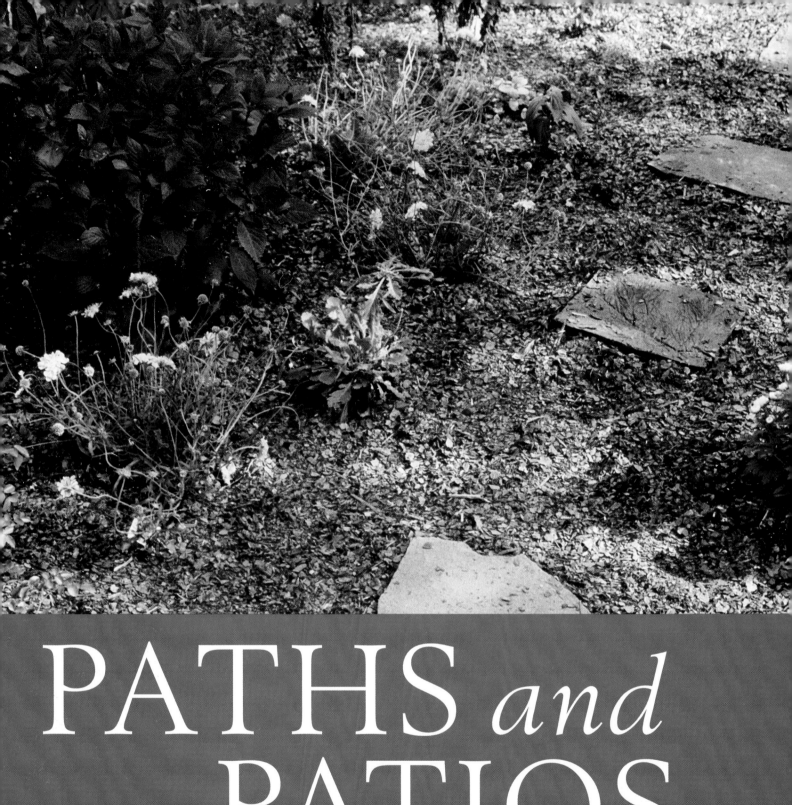

PATHS *and* PATIOS

2

IN ANY GARDEN THERE NEEDS TO be a way for one to walk through the space. Whether on a mulch bark path or a brick walkway, paths give the garden cohesiveness and create moods. Brick walkways bespeak formality while pine needles or stepping stones feel more relaxed and informal. What moods do you want to establish in your garden? A sense of mystery with a curved path? A point of destination with a straight walk to a gazebo?

Designing paths isn't all that complicated if you follow the design principles shared here. And don't worry that you'll need to hire a professional to install a walkway or patio. We'll show you how to do it yourself or, at the very least, give you the information you need to talk with a professional.

GORDON HAYWARD

is a garden designer, lecturer, and writer in Putney, Vermont. He and his wife have led garden tours in England and Ireland.

Paths
Establish Cohesiveness and Style

Connect the different areas in your yard or garden with a series of paths. Well-designed paths create a mood such as this natural stone path that has a relaxed feeling suitable to a woodland setting.

THINK OF YOUR GARDEN as a novel. Each planted area is a chapter with its own mood, cast of characters, and purpose. The path is your novel's theme or main character. It runs through everything, linking the chapters to tell a unified story. Just as a strong lead character is central to a good book, strong paths are central to good garden design. They provide structure and cohesion in a garden.

Paths also define your garden's itinerary. Well-designed paths are irresistible—they invite, even pull, guests into the garden. Put a curve in a path that disappears around a corner and your guests will follow it to see what's around the bend. Then, let the path lead to another garden and yet another, always varying the nature of the paths and their adjacent gardens, and you will create a place of intrigue, surprise, movement, and variety.

31

Curved paths create an element of surprise.

in your design, it should be distinguished with planted pots, lighting, and a richly planted entrance garden.

A secondary and thus narrower path, perhaps of stepping stones or brick, might run along or through gardens across the front of your house or down either side. Tertiary, and therefore even narrower, paths made of crushed gravel, bark mulch, or pine needles might run off the secondary paths into woodlands, to the compost pile, or to the gate of a fenced vegetable garden.

PAVING MATERIALS DEFINE A PATH

With the hierarchy of paths comes a hierarchy of paving materials. Bluestone and other geometric paving stones are highest. They are best for formal, wide, straight paths, such as those leading to the front door. Primary paths can also be made of brick, next down in the hierarchy. Following brick in descending order of formality are straight-edged, fieldstone paths; lawn; concrete; stepping stones; wooden bridges, boardwalks and ramps; hard, loose materials such as crushed gravel and peastone; and soft, loose materials like bark mulch, pine needles, leaves, and trodden earth. Establishing a relationship of paving material to path prominence is a major step toward successful garden design.

Once you determine the locations, widths, and paving materials for your paths, you can then see each of them as the spine of a new garden. Here's an example: Run a straight, cut-stone path from your back terrace steps 50 feet to an existing or planned group of trees or a summerhouse at the back of your lawn. Once you have the path in, envision it as the spine of a lush perennial garden planted on both sides of the path. Or picture the

CREATE A HIERARCHY OF PATHWAYS

In designing paths, it's helpful to think about them in terms of priority. Primary paths are the widest and most important, and often emanate from the most important doors of your house. The primary path is the one between your parking area and the front door. It might be made out of tightly fitting cut bluestone or sandstone. The widest path

This brick walkway instantly signals formality and leaves no doubt how the visitor is to travel through the garden.

grand effect of an allée of trees shading the path as it leads down to the summerhouse.

PATHS INVOKE MOODS

Paths create specific moods for garden visitors. A meandering pine-needle path through a spruce woodland is calming. A bark-mulch path through a vegetable garden feels practical and matter-of-fact. A straight and finely edged, 8-foot-wide lawn path between two perennial beds bespeaks elegance and formality. You can manipulate these moods by the way you create the paths. For example, lay a 5-foot-wide, straight brick path from the sidewalk to the front door using new, machine-made brick and you create a formal path that calls for formal gardens on either side. Lay that same path with old brick and

A gate at the end of the path signals a transition to another garden space.

A gazebo at the end of the path provides a sense of destination.

Tall trees screen the upcoming view and provide a sense of mystery.

Repetitive plantings draw the eye down the path and create a sense of rhythm.

A wide path of grass invites visitors to stroll slowly through the garden.

> *"Establishing a relationship of paving material to path prominence is a major step toward successful garden design."*

you relax the feeling of both the path and the adjacent beds. Narrow and curve the path, set the old bricks well apart to make room for small ground-hugging plants like thyme, and you further underpin its informal design, creating a path that might run through a casual herb garden.

A path is certainly a means of getting from point A to point B. But paths in a well-designed plan are much more—they invite us in to explore and to enjoy the varied beauty of our gardens.

Plants spilling over or growing between stairs add to their sense of informality.

A narrow path of stone invites visitors to explore other garden areas.

Pathway Design

Principles

JOE PARKS

gardens in Dover, New Hampshire, where he has built more than ¼ mile of paths and planted more than a thousand rhododendrons.

Flowering annuals and perennials along a winding grass path pull the viewer forward in anticipation of the pleasures to come.

WHY DO YOU ENJOY visiting some gardens more than others? The secret often lies underfoot. In the most alluring gardens, the paths that you tread—whether they're made of bricks, stones, grass, or mulch—have been carefully laid out to lead you through the garden and reveal its beauty.

Paths are one of the most important elements in a garden. First and foremost, they're a practical necessity for getting around the garden and for guiding visitors through it. But paths also provide a framework—a skeleton, if you like—that links the elements of a garden together, making the total more than the sum of its parts. And paths affect the way you view a garden; a well-designed path creates anticipation for what lies ahead and focuses attention on the garden's best features.

You don't have to be a landscape architect to design an effective path. I'm an amateur gardener with no special

Evergreen plantings conceal what's around the curve.

The gray gravel contrasts with the rhododendrons, drawing attention to them.

Use gravel as an informal and low-maintenance material.

training—just 50 years of experience. After considerable study, much trial, and many errors, I've found that a few basic principles make a path both practical and artful.

CREATE MYSTERY WITH CURVES

A path that curves is inviting. A straight path, particularly in a small garden, leaves little to the imagination; if we can see everything all at once, we feel less inclined to move through a garden. But a winding path obscures the distant view and thus piques our curiosity. We wonder what we might find around the bend. Even if your path has only one gentle curve, your visitors will feel encouraged to investigate and enjoy the pleasure of guessing what comes next.

You need to conceal from the eye what lies beyond a curve. Sometimes the terrain will help; sometimes existing trees or shrubs will provide a reason for a curve. Usually, though, you'll have to arrange plantings to block the view. I use evergreen shrubs such as rhododendrons and hollies to make my curves blind.

LEAD WITH PLEASURES, INVITE PAUSES

Around a curve, offer something to attract the eye and entice the viewer to take a closer look. A glimpse of a flower bed or a bench draws visitors along a path and rewards their journey. My garden path winds in and out through my large collection of rhododendrons. To avoid monotony, I planted many small beds of perennials, along with small trees and shrubs along the path, each designed to provide a special attraction at some time during the year—a mass of primulas or gentians, a bed of astilbes, a witch hazel.

Give your path a destination: a place to sit, a special view, or just a loop that leads back—few of us like to find we've arrived at a dead end.

It's one thing to get visitors to start down a path but another to get them to pause and enjoy what surrounds them. Here's where subtlety in path design comes into play. Like pools of water along a rushing stream, occasional wider sections in a path encourage people to slow their pace. On the other hand, straight, narrow sections in a path encourage visitors to keep moving. Simply by controlling the width of a path, you can modulate the mood of your garden from energetic to restful.

You can also use steps to slow people down and to increase variety along the path. My garden has very little slope, but I've built steps where I want visitors to look around.

"A well-designed path creates anticipation for what lies ahead and focuses attention on the garden's best features."

For two people to walk abreast comfortably, a path should be at least 4 feet wide; for people to walk single file it should be 2 feet wide. Steps should be at least 4 feet wide, for safety and to allow plants to trail over the edges.

USE AN APPROPRIATE MATERIAL

The materials you use for your paths also have an effect on how visitors view your garden. A straight brick walk and a meandering moss path create entirely different impressions.

Billowing plantings along a pine-needle path vary the width of the passage. On all garden paths, visitors tend to pause in wide sections and to keep moving in narrow sections.

The uniform curve, neat edges, and smooth surface of a brick path combine to make an inviting, formal approach to the front door at its end.

plants along the edge of the path to soften the hard lines.

Properly installed, bricks, concrete pavers and cut stones require little maintenance and are easy to walk on. But they are relatively expensive and require skill to install.

In a natural-looking, informal setting, choose materials that recall paths found in nature, such as moss, gravel, or mulch. The mood they create is restful and casual; they invite the visitor to enjoy the garden at leisure.

CONSIDER MAINTENANCE WHEN CHOOSING MATERIALS

Materials for informal paths tend to be much less expensive to purchase and are more easily installed than materials for formal paths. Choose grass, moss, or dirt, and I promise you'll get plenty of "oohs" and "ahs"—but you'll also have plenty of maintenance. Grass must be mowed and weeded. It grows poorly in shade. Worst of all, it won't stay put; you'll have to keep it carefully edged or in a trice you'll have grass popping up among your choice perennials. Moss tolerates shade and requires no mowing, but it hates foot traffic and needs constant weeding. Dirt is the most natural of all path materials, but even when earth is carefully pounded down, rain (or irrigation water) quickly turns it soft or muddy. It also serves as an open invitation to grass and weeds.

In my experience, the best choices for an informal path are natural stone, gravel, or mulch. One of the most elegant informal paths you can have is natural stepping stones surrounded by moss. Stepping stones should be as large as you can easily handle; stones less than 12 inches across in any direction soon become unstable and make for uncomfortable walking.

There is a variety of materials that can be used to build paths. Concrete, brick, stone, concrete pavers, gravel, mulch, grass, dirt, moss—alone or in combination—all make fine paths. In deciding what to use, consider the mood you wish to create as well as cost, installation, and maintenance.

Because of their straight, uncompromising lines, concrete, brick, concrete pavers, and cut stone paths are best suited to a formal garden. But you can integrate them into an informal garden by curving the path and varying its width so that it looks more like a country lane. It also helps to plant trailing

I particularly like gravel paths. They are easy to make, need little maintenance, and, once packed down, are easy to walk on. I use ¼- or ⅜-inch bank-run, washed gravel for my paths. Larger gravel is difficult to walk on. Gravel paths should be at least 2½ feet wide because plants along the edge inevitably spread into them.

Mulches such as bark, wood chips, and pine needles make unobtrusive, dry paths.

But mulches are slow to pack down and become walkable, they break down quickly, and they tend to have poorly defined edges that require marking, lest feet wander off course.

Whatever material you choose, remember that a path is more than a means of getting around without stepping on plants. With a little forethought, you can design paths that will make it a pleasure to visit your garden.

Trailing perennials planted along the edge of a cut-stone path soften its sharp edges, an appropriate touch for an informal garden.

A path of stepping stones surrounded by moss meanders over a dry stream bed in a woodland garden. The stones appear to have been arranged by nature, belying their careful placement by the author.

VINCENT LAURENCE

designs and installs gardens in southwestern Connecticut, focusing primarily on rustic yet elegant planting schemes and custom-built structures.

Choosing Pavers *for the* Garden

Random flagging provides places for plants, which add character and help to soften the stone visually.

I BOUGHT MY FIRST HOME about two years ago, a funky old barn that was converted to a house in the '70s. The rusticity of the place is somewhat refined, however, thanks to the good taste and hard work of its previous owner. Beside the house he put in a number of Japanese maples, dwarf conifers, and flowering shrubs that follow a long, sweeping staircase leading to the main entrance at the rear of the house. Time, unfortunately, has begun to take its toll on these stairs: The painted timber risers that define the steps are crumbling and splitting in places, and even the ones that look intact sound suspiciously hollow when kicked.

Last summer I started thinking about replacing these steps. Bluestone and brick came to mind immediately. I wanted a classic look, some combination of materials both ancient and ageless, that would be in keeping with the character of the barn and its gardens.

WHAT'S OUT THERE?
AN OVERVIEW

I didn't want to limit the scope of my search prematurely, so I took a look at the entire range of segmental pavers, as these materials are called in the industry. Besides brick and stone, there are also interlocking concrete pavers, some of which are fair imitations of natural stone. As I talked with suppliers and manufacturers of these materials, it quickly became evident that almost every gardener or homeowner thinking about putting in a path or patio has the same questions: How long will a particular material last? What colors is it available in? How much does it cost? And, can I install it myself?

The short answer to the first question is that all of these materials will last a long time—from perhaps 20 or 30 years to many

centuries—longer, anyway, than most people own their homes these days.

The number of color options for these materials varies, with brick having the fewest, though still far more than you might imagine. There's no shortage of choices.

The cost of the materials varies tremendously, from less than $2 a square foot on up to $30 a square foot for some exotic slates and limestones from Asia and South America. Prices aren't always quoted per square foot, though. Rather, you may be told how much a material costs by the piece (bricks, cobbles, and concrete pavers are sold this way) or by the ton (as with flagstone, for example).

As for doing it yourself, all of the suppliers and landscape professionals I spoke with agreed that a reasonably handy person—

Old, mossy, weathered bricks belong in a cottage garden. At the same time ancient and ageless, old brick is the perfect complement to a cottage garden's lush, unrestrained abandon.

as gardeners usually are—can handle putting in a path or small patio. As a rule, the more regular or uniform a paving material is, the easier it is to install. The more irregular—especially in thickness—the greater the challenge.

Ultimately, your choice of paving material will come down to your tastes and budget.

ALL BRICKS
ARE NOT CREATED EQUAL

I went looking for a brick with soul, one that looked like it would be at home in a grand, old English garden and that would age gracefully, acquiring a mossy, weathered patina. What I found, for the most part, was something else entirely. Almost all of the paver brick that I saw in catalogs, stoneyards, and masonry supply stores had a uniform, commercial look. One of the reasons for this is that much or most of it is extruded—that is, squeezed through a machine, like toothpaste out of a tube.

It's available in many colors, from honey-tan to a deep red with black, called flash red. Stops along the way include rose, pink, and many shades of red. Paver bricks are available in different thicknesses and with various edge treatments (such as beveled edges) as well.

In terms of strength and durability, these modern paver bricks are very consistent. Any brick that wants to call itself a paver has to meet government-mandated criteria for compression strength and water absorption. This ensures consistent wearing and a neat, homogenous look. For a slightly rougher look, these bricks are also sold tumbled, which chips and softens the edges. Because of the additional labor, these cost a bit more.

Modern bricks should last practically forever—more than a lifetime anyway. And because they're of a uniform size, bricks are

Extruded paver brick, black.

Tumbled extruded paver brick, red flash.

Contemporary molded brick, red.

Salvaged brick, red.

one of the easier materials to work with. They're also among the least expensive paver options. In a more contemporary garden than mine, these bricks may be ideal.

I wanted pavers with character, so I kept looking. After talking with brick manufacturers all over the country, I finally found one

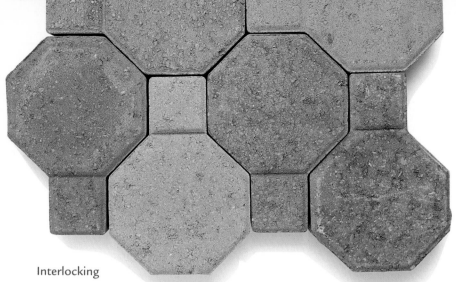

Interlocking concrete pavers come in a huge range of shapes, sizes, and colors.

Tumbled concrete paver with face mix, natural.

company in Bridgewater, Massachusetts, that still makes brick pavers that look like they could have been made 100 years ago. V. Stiles & Hart has, as it turns out, been making brick since 1893. Then I heard about another company that's been making bricks for more than 100 years—St. Joe Brick Works in Pearl River, Louisiana. So, there are a few companies out there still making old-fashioned paving brick. You've just got to look for them.

I wondered, too, about salvaged brick. It's old, and unlike many vintage materials, it costs no more than new. I'd heard that it shouldn't be used for paving, however—that it wouldn't last. That's because it's quite likely that salvaged brick is structural brick, originally used on the interior of a building behind a tougher, more weather-resistant veneer brick. Structural bricks were not "hard-fired," a term that refers to the temperature and duration of the firing that cures the brick. As a result, they absorb moisture more readily, making them more prone to spalling (chipping or flaking) than veneer or paver bricks.

One brick manufacturer told me candidly, however, that though salvaged brick isn't as consistently tough as the newer brick pavers, it's probably just fine for a residential garden path.

"In ten years," he said, "you might have to replace a few bricks. Big deal." There's no such thing as a maintenance-free garden.

THIS ISN'T YOUR FATHER'S CONCRETE

Concrete pavers made their way from Europe to the United States in the late 1970s, but didn't really catch on here until just five or six years ago. Since then their sales have jumped an average of 10 percent each year. Now they're everywhere. One landscape architect told me every time he uses concrete pavers on a job, another potential client sees them and wants them.

They come in a lot of different shapes—squares, rectangles, triangles, octagons with tails, you name it. There are even concrete pavers that are shaped like bricks. According to the industry organization, the Interlocking Concrete Pavement Institute, they're supposed to last 30 years. There are plenty of examples of Roman concrete work still in existence after nearly 2,000 years, so I'd guess that 30 years is a pretty conservative estimate.

As for color, granulated or liquid pigments are added to cement and aggregate to produce these pavers, so the available palette is essentially infinite. Earth tones are what you'll find most commonly, though. Some are available tumbled or with a preweathered finish to give them a headstart on a patina. Along with brick, concrete pavers are also one of your least expensive options.

Most concrete pavers look quite institutional or commercial to me, which is not surprising. They're being aggressively marketed as a pavement (asphalt or concrete) replacement, and are being used for airport taxiways, streets, sidewalks, and city squares.

But in addition to the more commercial-looking pavers, there are a few varieties I've seen that really look great and that would be right at home in a cottage garden or weaving their way through perennial borders. Unlike most other concrete pavers, this type has a "face mix" of fine sand and cement over a core of cement and coarser aggregate. The result is a paver with a surface that's so much smoother than the other concrete pavers that it almost looks like natural stone.

A STONE FOR EVERY TASTE AND NEED

The stoneyard I visited had more than 1,000 different types of stone on hand—different kinds of cobblestones, sandstone, limestone, granite, quartzite, and on and on. Walking into a yard like this can set your head spinning—but it doesn't have to. All these varieties of stone can be reduced to two basic categories: regular (think square or rectangular) and irregular, or free-form. These aren't official categories, but it's how most potential garden-masons describe stone when they visit a supplier, and it provides a useful framework for discussing what would otherwise be an unwieldy spectrum.

Within the regular or squarish category, there are cobblestones and pavers. Although many a street has been paved with cobble-

"When you go to the stoneyard, you should be ready to show or describe the look you're after."

stones, they're not technically considered pavers. The most familiar type of cobblestone is the granite Belgian block. They're commonly available in two sizes—regulation (4 x 5 x 9 inches) and jumbo (4 x 7 x 11 inches), though other sizes do exist. Colors vary with supplier, but gray and rose-pink are available almost everywhere. Belgian blocks—being granite—will last centuries.

Cobblestones are also sometimes available in limestone. There are many different varieties of limestone, though, so it's difficult to say anything meaningful about its durability. Some are very soft, but other types are nearly as hard as granite. If you see limestone cobbles you like, ask how they'll wear.

Pavers, the other type of regularly shaped stone, make up the largest category of stone. Pavers are classified either as random rectangular or cut-to-size. Random rectangular, an industry classification, is defined as stone between 12 inches square and 24 inches by

Granite Belgian block cobblestone, gray.

Limestone cobblestone, white.

36 inches, in graduations of 6 inches in either dimension. Anything else with 90-degree corners is considered cut-to-size.

Either way, pavers are generally split along the grain out of larger pieces of rock, so they have cleft faces, top and bottom. Pavers vary in thickness, but for footpaths, patios, and the like, 1½ inches is plenty thick. Pavers are available in a wide range of stones including (but not limited to) various kinds of limestone, quartzite, slate, granite, and sandstone. Prices vary by material. The most popular type of paver material is bluestone, which is a kind of sandstone.

Despite its name, bluestone ranges in color from brown to blue and includes virtually every hue in between, including rusty grays, lavender, and more. Color ranges can generally be specified, but the pickier you get, the pricier it gets. Tumbled bluestone is also available from some suppliers. These stones have softened edges that are intended to look like they've been around for a few centuries. With some thyme coming up through the cracks and a season of foot traffic, they could be convincing. More labor has gone into producing them, so you'll pay a bit more.

In terms of durability, bluestone falls in the middle of the pack. It's highly variable, though, depending both on the stone (bluestone is quarried in many different areas) and on the climate in which it's used. The harsher the winters, the shorter the life of the stone. A 20-year-old patio in Vermont will probably be showing signs of wear and may even have a few spalled pavers that could use replacing. On the West Coast, the same patio might last four or five times as long.

The other main category of stone is flagstone, or natural flagging, which simply

Bluestone paver, blue.

Bluestone paver, lavender.

Bluestone paver, predominantly rust.

Tumbled bluestone paver, blue.

means that its edges are irregular. Flagstone is generally available in the same stones that cut pavers are, as well as in fieldstone, a generic category for stone composed of various minerals—the mutt of the paving world. Flagstone is split to thickness as pavers are, but it doesn't always split as cleanly. As a result, it's more difficult to lay than most of the other materials. Again, the price depends on the stone you choose.

PREPARE BEFORE YOU GO TO BUY STONE

A little preparation before you head off to the stoneyard with checkbook in hand will go a long way toward making it a smooth experience. First off, you should have a rough sketch of the area you intend to pave—a basic site plan—with dimensions.

If you'd like some help in choosing an appropriate material, bring along photos of your house, gardens, and especially the area that you'll be paving. You should think

about, and be ready to show or describe, the kind of look that you're after. Finally, bring along any photos from books, magazines, or catalogs that will help you to communicate your vision.

So what did I end up doing with my steps? Well, let's just say that a bad case of sticker shock delayed the project. Maybe later this year.

Vermont slate flagstone, red.

Limestone flagstone.

Quartzite flagstone.

A small patio of concrete pavers provides a focal point in this garden room.

S. ANDREW SCHULMAN

is a Seattle-based land-
scape designer, garden
writer, and photographer.
He lectures frequently on
rose gardening and gar-
den design.

A Concrete *Garden* Path

Poured concrete can be
molded into almost
any shape, including
the curve needed to
reach the author's
front door.

PEOPLE OFTEN SCOFF at concrete as a
paving material for gardens. After all, it's ugly,
utilitarian, and cheap, right? Well, you'd better think again. Not only is concrete among
the most durable of paving options, it's also
versatile, economical, and, when used with taste and
imagination, downright beautiful. Modern concrete
offers so many options for color, pattern, and texture that
I didn't consider any other material when it came time to
replace the eroding path that led to our front door.

Concrete paths are either poured in place or set as
factory-made precast units. Ready-made concrete pavers
are typically molded and colored to imitate brick, stone,
or even wood. What poured concrete offers over factory-
made pavers and the materials they imitate is flexibility.
With proper engineering, poured concrete can be molded
into almost any shape—including the abrupt curve

Today's concrete offers many options for color, pattern, and texture. On this path you can see an exposed aggregate surface that's edged with raked concrete.

Don't feel constrained by concrete. Any number of designs, from simple raked patterns to the stone inlays shown above, can be incorporated into a concrete walk.

To prevent cracking, concrete walks need expansion joints every few feet. In mild climates you can use treated lumber, which adds decorative contrast to any path.

required to get to my front door. There are only a few strictures. The concrete must be poured to an adequate thickness for the local climate and the weight it has to bear. The ground beneath the path must also be properly compacted. Paths that are especially complex in shape or subject to heavy loads may require steel reinforcing bars ("rebar") cast into their interior.

I designed my own path with the two basic components of concrete firmly in mind: Portland cement and aggregate. Portland cement is the "glue" that holds concrete together: a mixture of crushed lime and clays that is heated, ground, and mixed with water. Aggregate is the loose material that gives concrete its bulk and strength; it can include sand, gravel, and crushed rock. The choice and treatment of these two components would determine the look and feel of my new front walk.

CONCRETE COMES IN A RANGE OF COLORS AND TEXTURES

Portland cement comes in a range of colors, from the familiar light gray to various shades of beige, tan, slate, and russet. If you're finicky, as I am, you can also custom tint the cement for a particular paving job. For my path, I chose a soft, bluish gray that contrasts gently with the yellow paint on my house and makes a fine foil for many different colors of flowers and foliage.

I also chose an exposed aggregate surface. In most cases the upper surface of a concrete path is a fine-textured coating of Portland cement and sand. But this relatively smooth layer can be washed off with a jet of water before it sets, leaving the aggregate visible at the surface. The effect is much like a gravel

path but with greater firmness and stability. The color, size, and shape of the exposed aggregate determine the appearance and the texture of the path.

I used aggregate containing many rounded pebbles, ¼ inch in diameter. Their colors are an assortment of tans and dark grays that contrast subtly with the tinted Portland cement. The surface they create offers gentle traction during winter rains and a lively but unobtrusive play of color in the sunlight.

CONCRETE WALKS CAN HAVE ELABORATE DESIGNS

Forgoing exposed aggregate does not mean doing without surface interest. As any mischievous 12-year-old can tell you, a partially set concrete surface makes a wonderful canvas. Don't feel constrained by the average prankster's repertoire of hearts and footprints. Any number of designs, from simple brushed or raked patterns to elaborately carved lines and figures, can be incised into a concrete walk.

You may also want to consider inset stones, heavy-duty tiles, or colored glass. On their own or in combination, inset materials and carved patterns can turn a concrete path into a work of art. Do make sure to smooth the ends of any incised lines to prevent jagged edges, as these can be both messy and dangerous. To reduce the danger of tripping, keep any carving or inlay near the edges of the path, rather than the more heavily trafficked center.

Since concrete combines beautifully with many other paving materials, it's worth considering an edging of brick or stone to demarcate your path. A band of loosely set, rounded stones makes a particularly nice transition between the concrete path and planted areas.

Concrete can be tinted
(as shown here),
scored, or texturized. —

Plants spilling onto the
path soften the edges. —

An edging of brick,
stone, or tile marks
your path and creates
an interesting pattern. —

You might also edge your walk with an additional band of concrete—perhaps with a contrasting tint or surface treatment. Or you may prefer to allow low-growing plants to creep and spill onto the path, giving it a soft, indefinite edge.

EXPANSION JOINTS WILL PREVENT CRACKING

Concrete walks of any length will require expansion joints every few feet to prevent cracking. Luckily, the oozy, black, tar-soaked joints you tried to avoid stepping on as a child are a thing of the past. Fiber-based, polyurethane foam, epoxy, and rubberized expansion joints are now made in a variety of colors and are much less likely to ooze in the summer heat. Seattle's mild winters allowed me to use treated-lumber expansion joints, whose lines add decorative contrast to the path.

That's just one example of how new technologies or a creative approach can turn the engineering requirements of concrete into a decorative asset. So the next time you plan a new garden path, consider concrete. It's not just a workhorse, and it's certainly not ugly. Banish any images of crumbling urban sidewalks, and recognize concrete for what it is: the most adaptable, sculptural, and permanent of garden paving materials.

"The color, size, and shape of the exposed aggregate determine the appearance and the texture of the path."

PHYLLIS GORDON

has retired from two
careers and now lives in
Florida, where her new
passion is tropical plants.

To Build
a Brick Garden
Path

If you played with
blocks as a kid, you
can build a brick path
as an adult. The actual
laying of the bricks is
the easy part. Digging
an 8-inch-deep trench
for the underlying
layers of gravel and
sand is what takes the
most time.

WHEN I MOVED FROM New
England to Maryland, I was struck
by all the brickwork. There are
brick houses, brick sidewalks, and
brick paths to the brick barns. Even
the streets in some of the towns are paved with brick.
Because of the warmth of its color, the strength of its
material, and the good feeling underfoot, my desire was
born; someday I would have a brick sidewalk.

I spoke of it so often that one day I came home to find
300 old, handmade bricks tossed in a pile in my yard, a
gift from a friend who said, "You wanted them. Now
use them."

There was no turning back. As I stacked the bricks, I
began to wonder how on earth to begin such an ambitious project. Well, you look at your yard and lay garden
hoses along the edges of the path-to-be, moving the hoses
around until the curve and location please your eyes and

Calculating Materials for a Brick Path

A garden hose is the perfect flexible tool for planning the curves and sweeps of your brick path, but it might be hard to measure the length of your path after you determine its circuitous route. Mark how much of the hose you used in your layout, then simply pull the hose out straight and measure the length. Multiply the length of the hose by the path width you want. This gives you the total square feet of the path.

GRAVEL

You'll need a 4-inch-deep layer (or 0.3333 feet) of gravel for your path's foundation trench. Multiply the total square feet of your path by 0.3333. This will give you the cubic feet of gravel you need. If your gravel supplier wants cubic yards, divide the cubic feet by 27.

HEAVY-DUTY WEED-BARRIER FABRIC

You'll need enough fabric to cover the total square footage of your path. Because you'll have to overlap the edges, figure on buying an extra 15 percent.

SAND

The layer of sand in the foundation is 2 inches deep, but you'll need extra sand to set the soldier bricks along the edges and to sweep into the spaces between the bricks. Multiply the total square footage of the path by 0.25 to determine the cubic feet of sand you'll need.

BRICKS

A good rule of thumb is that you'll need four-and-a-half bricks per square foot of path. You'll also need six soldier bricks for each linear foot of path.

It goes without saying that gravel, sand and bricks are heavy. This is the reason suppliers usually have a delivery charge—sometimes as high as $50. Make sure you ask before you contract to buy materials.

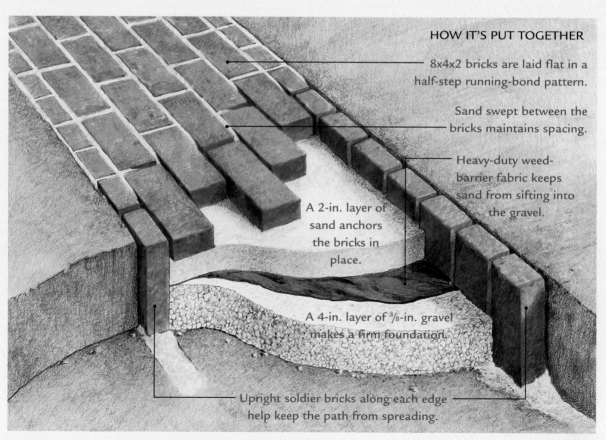

HOW IT'S PUT TOGETHER

8x4x2 bricks are laid flat in a half-step running-bond pattern.

Sand swept between the bricks maintains spacing.

Heavy-duty weed-barrier fabric keeps sand from sifting into the gravel.

A 2-in. layer of sand anchors the bricks in place.

A 4-in. layer of 3/8-in. gravel makes a firm foundation.

Upright soldier bricks along each edge help keep the path from spreading.

"Remember—you're building a brick garden path, and it's a process that's more organic than exacting."

you have a place to step on a rainy day. It's best to put the path where you normally walk. It will look just right, and it will keep you on track and out of the mud.

My path would be 2 feet wide, and along each edge I would run a course of bricks standing upright like sentinels, keeping their laid-flat fellows in line.

Still, I was a long way off from laying the first brick. Had I known how far away that moment would be, I might have given up.

THERE'S LOTS OF WORK BEFORE THE FIRST BRICK IS LAID

A proper brick path has to be set on a good foundation of 4 inches of gravel, a layer of heavy-duty weed-barrier fabric, and then 2 inches of sand. The fabric lets water through, but it keeps the sand from sifting into the gravel.

I wanted the top of the 2-inch-thick bricks to be even with the ground level. The thickness of the brick, combined with the sand and gravel layers, meant I'd need to dig a trench 8 inches deep for the length of the path. So, I picked up my spade, started to dig, and quickly ran smack into the next question. What would I do with all this topsoil? Digging an 8-inch-deep, 2-foot-wide trench 50 feet long makes almost 2½ cubic yards of dirt—about 50 full wheelbarrows.

Mine was an easy answer. In the first 90 years of its life, my house had no gutters. Water running off the eaves washed away soil until too much foundation was bare and left swales under the roof's drip line. I wanted garden beds under the eaves, and the beds needed lots of topsoil. Someone else might want soil for raised beds or to fill in holes. There is always a use for topsoil as long as you know it's coming.

Every day that spring and summer, I shoveled out the bed of the path-to-be and hauled dirt around my house. By now, the first pile of sand—I'd use it to set the brick soldiers— stood waiting in the backyard, and I had trundled my bricks in the wheelbarrow and stacked them neatly along the edge of the trench.

SET THE SOLDIER BRICKS, ADD GRAVEL AND SAND

I learned many things those months: that I could wheelbarrow only 20 bricks at a time, that they measure about 8x4x2 inches, and that they must be held upright along the path's edge by generous amounts of sand packed around them.

I found it best to dig a rough trench, line one side with the soldiers, go back to measure the width with a stick as long as the width of the path, then line the other side.

Weed-barrier fabric is laid between gravel and sand. The black fabric lets rainwater through, but it keeps the sand from settling into the gravel.

Lastly, after upright bricks lined both sides of the path, I adjusted the depth of the trench here and there with a flat shovel.

By now a fledgling mason, I discovered that I could use a trowel, straightedge, and level, all at the same time, then bop the bricks into their proper places with a rubber mallet. I got pretty good at it, too.

When the trench was done and the soldiers stood in line, it was time for the trucks to come with ⅜-inch gravel and palletized bricks (called "cubes"). I'd shopped the yellow pages under both "Sand and Gravel" and "Bricks" for prices and delivery info. The free bricks from my friend went only so far.

Visiting a few brick suppliers taught me that bricks come in different colors and prices, and that some bricks are more irregular than others. Irregular-shaped bricks are harder to lay in a pattern because of differences in their dimensions. High-fired paving bricks are the best for paths.

I hired two men to load the gravel into the trench and rake it smooth. It takes many wheelbarrow loads to make a 4-inch bed. When the gravel was all in place, I cut heavy-duty weed-barrier fabric into strips and laid it on the bed. A 2-inch layer of sand went on top of the gravel, raked smooth and leveled

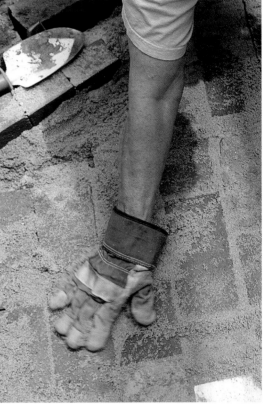

A rubber mallet won't break bricks, but it makes a great tool for persuading them into place. At left is a blue brick chisel used for cutting bricks.

Sand swept between the cracks keeps the spacing even between the bricks.

with a board pulled across its width. After the sand was leveled, the trench was ready. Finally, I could lay the 2-inch-thick bricks on top.

HALF-STEP RUNNING BOND IS AN EASY BRICK PATTERN TO LAY

Instead of a stylized pattern, like a herringbone or a basket weave, my bricks are laid in simple straight ahead lines that you see in most of the old pathways. The pattern—called a half-step running bond—is easy to remember, and the bricks are easy to manage. They fit nicely between their borders, even around gentle curves and sharp corners.

To start the pattern, you alternate a whole brick next to a half brick. A sharp blow with a brick chisel and a 4-pound hammer cuts a brick in half. It takes some practice and gloves are a necessity. A miss with the hammer... I don't even want to remember.

As work, laying bricks was satisfying. I could see what I had done. As exercise, it was rewarding. I slimmed down one size.

Kneeling on a foam pad will save your knees. A rubber mallet bangs bricks in place without breaking them. Occasionally you have to shift a little sand under the brick, sprinkle some here and there to keep adja-

Warm colors and strong materials are part of the appeal of a brick path that winds through a garden.

White marble bricks mark the progress. Laying a brick path is hard work; the author builds 50 feet of new path every year.

cent brick edges even. A high corner will catch a snow shovel or a summer sandal.

MORE PATHS IN THE YEARS TO COME

When the last brick was down, I covered the whole length of the path with a thick layer of sand, sweeping it into the spaces between the bricks, adding more every couple of days for two weeks. Then I swept it clean, and my path was done.

After this first path, I was far from finished with my brick laying. The next spring, I started across the back of the house with a path to the deck. I do only 50 feet or so a season. I need time for social things and time to tend the gardens around my paths. In the coming years, I want a path from the deck to the shed.

By the way, if you live up north, in less temperate climates than the eastern shore of Maryland and want to build a brick path, you might want to tamp the sand and gravel with a power compactor from a tool rental store. The compactor settles the sand and gravel, and might prevent heaving when the ground freezes deep.

On a trip to Vermont, I found a quarry that cuts marble into bricks, so my walk has white marble scattered along its length. Not traditional, but I like it. Some are engraved with the year I finished a particular section, my personal log of the project.

SALLY ROTH

is a lifelong naturalist and gardener of New Harmony, Indiana, who writes and lectures about nature and plants. Her books include *Natural Landscaping* and *Attracting Hummingbirds and Butterflies*.

Make Your Own Stepping Stones

Create a paver of your own design. This cement paving stone has been tinted to blend with its slate neighbors.

ONE OF MY FAVORITE garden stepping-stones started life as the flat face of a sundial. When my rowdy spaniel galloped through, leaving a perfect paw print in the still-setting concrete, I had to scrap the sundial plans. But the 2-inch-thick disk was too good to waste, so I made it an unexpected find in the garden path.

Since that time, I've made stepping stones by design instead of by accident, a simple and gratifying project made easy with quick-setting concrete. Except for the concrete mix, most of the materials and tools can be found around the house. The only other requirements are a willingness to experiment and an appreciation of texture and pattern.

How many stones will you need? I follow the rose rule: Plant six lovely roses in a row and their beauty is diminished instead of multiplied. Place your stones sparingly.

1 Assemble your supplies. Purchase them at any well-stocked hardware store or home-supply center. Here's what you'll need:

- Quikrete mix
- straightedge
- bucket or wheelbarrow
- concrete dye
- petroleum jelly
- hoe
- decorations
- trowel
- heavy-duty rubber gloves
- form (cardboard box, strip of lath, etc.)
- dust mask

2 Grease the molds. Use petroleum jelly to make removal of the finished paving stones easier.

3 Don protective gear before handling Quikrete. You'll need a dust mask, long sleeves, pants, and some heavy-duty rubber gloves.

HOW TO MAKE YOUR OWN STEPPING-STONES

Like most of my successful projects, this one requires no special skills, and it offers almost instant gratification. The technique boils down to four steps: Mix the concrete (and dye, if you want a color other than gray), pour it, make decorative impressions or embed ornaments, and wait for it to dry.

Part of the fun for me is working with what I have. Instead of building a wooden form to specified dimensions, I use whatever's handy: aluminum lasagna pans or plastic trash-can lids, a strip of lath bent into a circle, even a pizza box. You can pour the concrete in place right in the garden, so the form, like a cookie cutter, doesn't need to have a solid bottom. Or you can pour the concrete directly into a free-form shape you've dug in the soil. Either way, dig out a section of soil to accommodate the finished paver to 1½ to 2 inches deep. Pour enough concrete to make the finished paver flush with the surrounding soil. A third alternative is to use a solid-bottom form, like a cardboard box or plastic pan. Think of it as a cake: Grease the pan, pour the batter, and remove when done.

4 Add water to your mixing container before you add any other ingredients.

5 Add dye to the water according to the instructions on the label.

6 Add Quikrete to the water. Stir the mixture with whatever is handy; a shovel or hoe work well. Be sure to rinse off tools immediately after use.

7 Aim for a consistency akin to cookie dough rather than to pancake batter—firm, not runny. Start with a smaller amount of water and add more as needed.

Stepping-stones should be about 1½ to 2 inches thick so that they bear weight without cracking. A 12- to 18-inch width is comfortable for most feet; you can cut a sheet of newspaper to find a good size and pleasing shape.

ASSEMBLING THE CONCRETE DETAILS

Plan the project for a dry day when the temperature is between 60°F and 70°F (cooler temperatures slow drying; hot air speeds it up and may cause cracking). For a small-scale project like this, you don't need a cement mixer to churn cement, gravel, sand, and water. All you need is a bag or two of quick-setting concrete mix, such as Quikrete. Quikrete comes in several formulas, so make sure to get the sand or concrete mix. Quick-setting concrete is quick indeed—you can walk on it in 30 minutes. It's the masonry equivalent of an instant cake mix: Just add water, stir, and pour. Be sure to wash all tools as soon as possible after using, before the concrete hardens on them.

Look for the small but heavy bags (40-, 60-, or 80-pound) at building-supply centers

8 Scoop or trowel the mix into waiting forms. Place the forms on a flat surface so that the pavers dry to an even thickness.

9 Have decorations at the ready. Look for foliage or flowers with distinctive rather than delicate shapes.

or hardware stores. Figure on 40 pounds of premix (about $5) for each 18-inch-square stepping stone. A 60-pound bag will cover a 2-foot square.

MAKING A GOOD IMPRESSION

Use a flat mason's trowel or the edge of a piece of scrap lumber to smooth the surface of your freshly poured paver. If you've used a mold with a solid bottom, you can lift it up and rap it on a hard surface to settle the con-

crete. Then add the decorations of your choice. Impressions in concrete should be deep enough to see, but shallow enough so that any water that collects after a rain will dry quickly. Deep impressions that hold water will lead to chipping and cracking, especially in cold-winter climates.

To embed bits of broken pottery or other accents, push them gently into the concrete surface until they are well anchored and level with the surface of the stone.

"Think of it as a cake: Grease the pan, pour the batter, and remove when done."

10 Press leaves into the pavers when the concrete is still damp. To get a clear image, press ornaments in firmly, then remove them.

11 Experiment with embellishment. Forget about color; just look at the form. If you don't like the effect, use your trowel or straightedge to erase the marks.

STEPPING ON A PLEASANT SURPRISE

I like to think of my special stepping stones as little secrets to tuck into a corner of the garden, waiting to be discovered. Not everyone will notice the subtle imprint of fern fronds—or dog paws—in the stones beneath their feet, but to those who do, and to the gardener who fashioned them, handmade paving stones are a very personal work of art that can be enjoyed every day.

Remove the pavers from the forms after about a half hour.

MARY ANNE CASSIN

is a landscape architect
with the Portland Parks
and Recreation
Department in Oregon.

A Dry-Laid
Paver
Patio

This patio serves as an outdoor gathering spot for relaxing and entertaining. It also acts as a transitional space between the house and the surrounding garden. The author and her husband designed and installed this patio themselves, using concrete pavers that give the look of stone at a fraction of the cost.

P UTTING IN A PATIO behind our new house was a high priority. My husband and I spend a lot of time outdoors gardening, but every now and then we like to sit back, relax, and admire the results of our labors. We also like to spend as much time as possible enjoying the Portland, Oregon, climate. Winters here are short, and the temperatures tend to remain above freezing. And summers are heavenly—consistently sunny but not hot or humid, ideal for dining and entertaining alfresco.

My husband is a landscape contractor and I am a landscape architect, so we had plenty of background in the technical skills that would be required for patio construction. These skills are not out of reach for the average home gardener, however. You can install a patio like ours if you do some research into materials and construction techniques.

A closer look at the patio gives a better idea of the sort of cutting required to fit a diagonal pattern into a rectangular space. The basalt cobble edging that Cassin and her husband used along the flower beds serves as a rustic complement to the more formal pavers.

PICK THE RIGHT SPOT

A flat spot on the north side of the house, accessible through the living room's French doors, seemed the natural spot to locate a patio. The yard and gardens frame this area on three sides. In a colder climate, a north-facing patio might not be usable for several months of the year, but because of our mild weather, we're able to use our patio year-round.

When deciding how big to make the patio, we considered the activities we wanted to take place there. We anticipated dinner parties and large gatherings of friends. We wanted room for a table and six chairs, with plenty of circulation space around them. We started by sketching things out on paper, including a rough drawing of the house and the yard and compass points. Laying out the future patio with stakes and string before we ordered any materials gave us a better feel for the shape, size, and location we'd chosen.

COMPARE PAVING MATERIALS

We began our search for a paving material by considering the traditional alternatives. None of them met our needs. We ruled out concrete and asphalt because a patio as large as ours (20 x 30 feet) would have required professional finish detailing to break up the monotony of these materials. Brick is attractive, relatively inexpensive, and durable, but it can be quite slippery in this climate because moss thrives on it. We liked the idea of a stone surface, but the cost turned out to be prohibitive.

We finally decided on precast concrete paving stones. A variety of paver styles and colors is available. The one we chose is called a "Roman paver." It has been tumbled, which roughens the edges, so it really does look like stone, especially when it's wet. Also, for some reason, moss doesn't grow on the pavers' surfaces; it only grows in the cracks. Finally, concrete pavers are meant to be dry-laid (laid on a bed of sand), so we didn't have to bother with the mess of mortar.

The cost met our objective and we don't have to worry about durability. The pavers are manufactured to withstand a pressure of 3,500 pounds per square inch. With proper base preparation, they can be used for roadway construction.

LAY A GOOD FOUNDATION

Successful installation of a dry-laid paver patio lies in proper preparation of the foundation on which the pavers rest. Accurate measurement and attention to construction details are important as you work on the layers of the sandwich: subbase (the ground beneath the patio), base (a layer of crushed rock), sand bed, and pavers. Just as important is the edging, which must be put in place around the perimeter of the patio before you begin paving. Because the pavers are dry-laid, they would soon shift without an edging to contain them.

ESTABLISH THE ELEVATION

We wanted the patio to follow existing grades as much as possible so that it would look like it belonged in its surroundings. We also made sure that the finished surface had a minimum slope of 2 percent (a drop of 6 inches over a 25-foot run) so water would drain off away from the house foundation. The patio could have had a greater slope than this, but your eye can determine a definite pitch at slopes of 4 percent or more. The closer the patio is to a house or other level surfaces, the more obvious the pitch. Our patio appeared level until we built a deck next to it; now the 2 percent slope is quite distinct.

We used a string level (also called a line level—a small level hooked onto a length of string) hung between stakes to mark out the elevation of the patio. We drove the stakes into the corners and studied the "givens" of the site. We knew what elevation we wanted the future deck to have, so we started by lev-

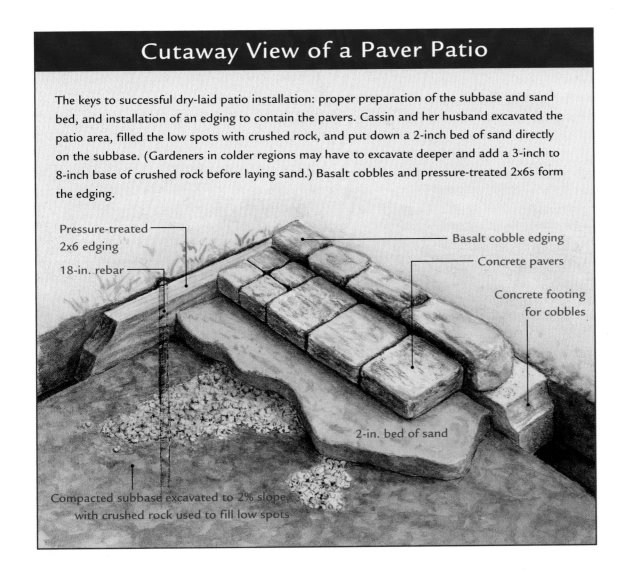

Cutaway View of a Paver Patio

The keys to successful dry-laid patio installation: proper preparation of the subbase and sand bed, and installation of an edging to contain the pavers. Cassin and her husband excavated the patio area, filled the low spots with crushed rock, and put down a 2-inch bed of sand directly on the subbase. (Gardeners in colder regions may have to excavate deeper and add a 3-inch to 8-inch base of crushed rock before laying sand.) Basalt cobbles and pressure-treated 2x6s form the edging.

Pressure-treated 2x6 edging

18-in. rebar

Basalt cobble edging

Concrete pavers

Concrete footing for cobbles

2-in. bed of sand

Compacted subbase excavated to 2% slope, with crushed rock used to fill low spots

eling the strings at that height. We also knew that the patio should slope to the west, in keeping with the existing grade. Since our patio was 30 feet wide in the direction of the slope, it had to have a minimum drop of 0.6 feet to achieve the required 2 percent grade (30 feet x .02 = 0.6 feet or $7\frac{3}{16}$ inches). To arrive at this slope, we dropped the string $7\frac{3}{16}$ inches down the stakes at the low end of the patio. We used the strings as guides to determine the depth of the subbase excavation.

INSTALLING THE EDGING

Although the manufacturers' brochures suggest preparing the subbase next, we decided to install the edging first to limit soil disturbance along the edge of the patio and to minimize damage to the lawn. The edging material can take many different forms: concrete curbs, wooden boards, strips of PVC, or steel bands. We chose a combination of stone and lumber.

We used split basalt cobbles as a prominent edge along the rock garden and annual beds. We mortared these in place on a 6-inch by 6-inch concrete footing (you may need a deeper footing in a colder climate). We wanted to minimize the visibility of the edging around the rest of the patio to give it a more open feel. Here we used pressure-treated 2 x 6s, setting them ½ inch below finished patio grade so that the deck, lawn and surrounding plants would conceal them later. The wood is held in place by concrete-reinforcement bars ("rebars"), which we purchased in 10-foot lengths from a lumberyard. We cut the rebars into 18-inch pieces with a hacksaw and pounded them in place on the outside of the wood every 5 feet or so.

PREPARING THE SUBBASE

The first step in preparing the subbase was to determine how deep to dig. To do this, we added the depth of the sand layer to be spread over the subbase (2 inches) to the thickness of the pavers. Then we subtracted this total from finished grade to find the elevation of the subbase.

Because our climate is mild and because we expected only foot traffic on our patio, it wasn't necessary to have any special base between the subbase and the sand bed. In colder climates, though, you may need to excavate 3 to 8 inches and fill the area with a base of crushed rock to reduce the chances of frost heave and settling. Check with the paver manufacturer or a local contractor to determine what sort of preparation is recommended in your area.

As we dug, we checked the depth at 6-inch intervals by measuring the distance from the ground to a string set at finished grade. We walked along the string with a tape measure and marked the high and low points with chalk, then moved the string and repeated the process. In this way, we were able to get a good idea of the size and shape of the bumps and the dips. We leveled the bumps with our shovels, and we filled in low spots with crushed, ¾-inch-minus rock (a mix of pieces no larger than ¾ inch). Only crushed rock will compact to the density required to provide a firm surface.

My husband and I spent the better part of a week, putting in a couple of hours every day, excavating and filling the low spots. We lifted the sod with spades (if you have to lift a lot of turf, consider renting a sod cutter) and removed the soil below with a flat, square-point shovel, checking the level as we went. (Call the electric and water utility companies before you begin to be sure that your digging won't damage underground cables or pipes.)

Once we arrived at the proper elevation, we compacted the subbase. We initially thought we could do a good enough job with a hand tamper, but we found that a motorized plate compactor (available from most rental companies) did a much better job. A plate compactor is noisy (ear plugs are a must) and heavy, but simple to operate. We ran it over the surface several times in each direction to be sure the material was adequately compacted.

It's important to get the subbase as level as possible (within ¼ inch) because the pavers

Dry-laid pavers rest on a bed of sand. The author and her husband leveled the sand to the correct depth with a screed, which they made by bolting two 10-foot 2x4s together. They notched the ends of the screed so that it hung down to the correct depth from the edging.

Cassin and her husband chose a pinwheel pattern set diagonally within a frame of pavers laid long side perpendicular to the edge. They used cardboard to space the pavers the recommended ⅛ inch apart until they discovered that the pavers were smashing the cardboard flat. They switched to ⅛-inch drill bits to finish the job.

will eventually settle to conform to the sub-base's contours. The plate compactor did not radically change the level of the excavation, but it did cause some uneven settling. We checked the grade again and added more gravel where necessary.

LAYING THE PAVERS

The paving itself took only two days, though they were long days. First, we spread the layer of sand on which the pavers rest. Our manufacturer recommended 2 inch; others may suggest as little as 1 inch. We then screeded the sand (leveled it with a straightedge). We built a special screed—two 10-foot-long 2x4s bolted together in the middle—to accommodate our large patio area. We notched the screed on either end so that it hung down to the desired level from the edging. Where we used the cobbles as an edging material, a board placed inside the stones served as a level guide.

It had already been a long day by the time we finished smoothing the sand. We pushed on because once the sand is down, it must not be disturbed until the pavers are in place, and we have pets who would have loved that huge litter box. So we spread all the sand and laid most of the pavers in one day, finishing up by floodlight at 11:30 p.m. We laid long planks over the rows of exposed sand to keep our pets at bay for the night.

Depending on your selection of pavers, there are several patterns to choose from: running bond, herringbone, and basket weave, among others. We chose a pattern that looks like a series of pinwheels, and set it on a diagonal to make it more dynamic. We bordered this pattern on all four sides with a row of pavers set perpendicular to the edge.

Placing the pavers wasn't difficult, but keeping them in line within the pattern was a little tricky. We started in a corner where the angle was exactly 90°, and kept a close eye on spacing, but we still found it necessary to start over more than once. The task was complicated by the need to leave a ⅛-inch gap between each paver on all sides. (Some manufacturers make pavers with built-in spacers.)

My husband had been skeptical about the wisdom of choosing a pattern that required the cutting of some 200 pavers, but the ease of using a brick saw allayed his concerns. The saw, which we also rented locally, is mounted on legs, so we could work standing up. Because the saw operates with a diamond blade under a constant stream of water, cutting the pavers was noisy and messy, but it was precise and quick. (Remember to wear safety goggles and ear plugs when operating a brick saw.) We were able to cut all the pavers (using chalk to mark the cuts), place them, and apply the finishing touches in time to dine on the patio the second day.

After placing the last pavers, we ran the plate compactor over the entire surface twice in both directions. This was horribly loud because of the hard surface. It brought out those neighbors who had not already been inspecting our progress.

The last part was easy and very satisfying. We swept dry sand over the surface (a wheelbarrow load is all we needed) to fill in the gaps between the pavers, and arranged the furniture and potted plants. We thought about christening the patio with a bottle of champagne but decided to drink it instead.

UPKEEP IS EASY

Our patio is now three years old and has lived up to our expectations in every way. We are happy to see the moss starting to fill in the cracks in the shadier corners, and we have fun experimenting with different arrangements of potted plants. Weeds do pop up in the cracks now and then, but they are easy to keep under control. The only other mainte-

"The only other maintenance required is an annual spring replenishment of sand swept into the cracks to replace that washed away by winter rains."

nance required is an annual spring replenishment of sand swept into the cracks to replace that washed away by winter rains.

We haven't noticed any significant settling or heaving, but if and when we do, repair will be simple. Since the pavers aren't mortared in place, all we have to do is lift the affected area, correct the base and re-lay the pavers.

The patio now looks as though it has always been there. With a treated hemlock deck connecting the patio to the house, we've created the perfect outdoor room from which to view our garden.

Once all of the pavers were laid, the patio was compacted, using a motorized plate compactor. Although heavy and noisy, it made compacting easy. The final job was sweeping a wheelbarrow load of dry sand into the cracks.

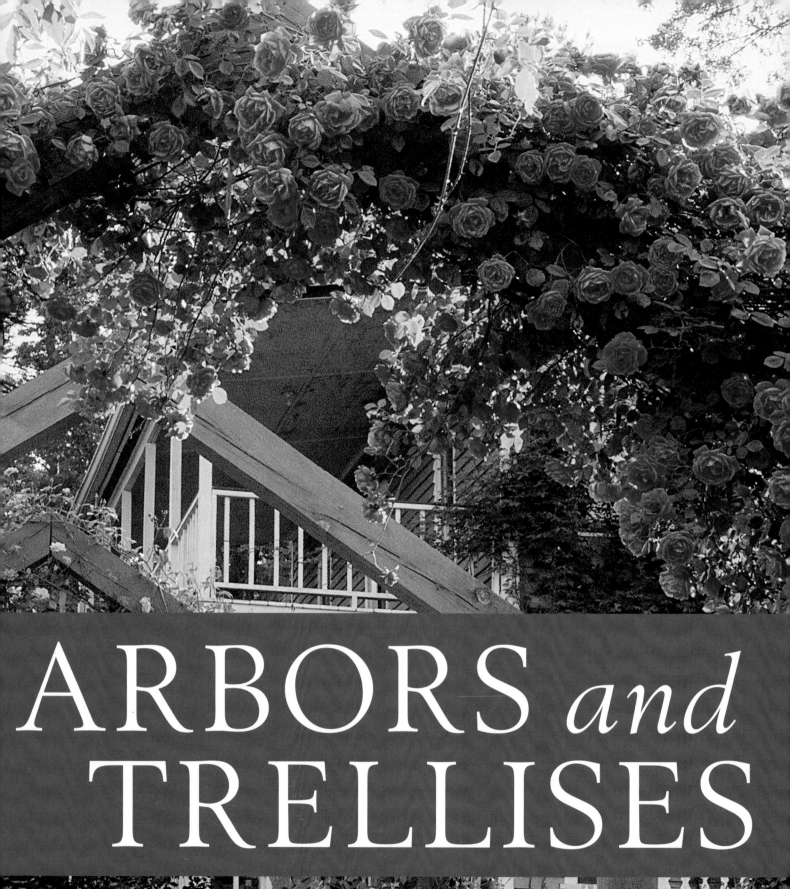

ARBORS *and* TRELLISES

3

ARBORS AND TRELLISES PROVIDE gardeners an opportunity to garden not just within the horizontal landscape, but also to expand into a vertical dimension—adding height and visual interest to the garden. Architecturally, they can serve as focal points to draw the eye or transition points from one garden to the next. But the most important thing about these structures—their raison d'être—is to support plants that want to climb—roses, wisteria, vines, morning glories, clematis. What gardener hasn't envisioned such a structure draped in their favorite flowers through which to walk or under which to sit?

Some plants are better suited to one structure over another. You'll learn which plants are ideal for each. And these structures don't need to be limited to formal wooden structures. We'll show you how to build trellises from copper and even sapling trees.

PAM BAGGETT

owns Singing Springs Nursery in Cedar Grove, North Carolina, specializing in uncommon tender plants and choice perennials.

Structures to Grow On

Choose substantial vines for substantial structures. An arbor or a pergola provides strong support for spirited climbers like wisteria, trumpet creeper, and grapevines.

PERHAPS YOU LOVE the look of vines, or maybe you've filled your garden to the point that there's no place to go but up. In either case, when you decide to plant a vine, what should you grow it on? From rustic cedar posts to elegant wrought-iron pergolas, gardeners have many choices for sending plants skyward. Still, making a perfect match between your vine, its support, and the surrounding scenery requires careful consideration.

I like to think of my vines and their supports as wrestlers involved in a battle for dominance. Before I do any planting, I research the vines to determine if they will be balanced in size and strength with whatever structure I'm training them on. For example, I was unsuccessful in my attempt to lure *Mandevilla* × *amoena* 'Alice du Pont' up an 8-foot post one summer. Now I understand why it is that I usually see this slow grower bedecking mailboxes instead.

TRELLISES ARE FOR TWINERS

Trellises offer an excellent means of adding vines to the garden. Whether made from wood or plastic, these cross-hatched structures can be placed behind flower beds to provide a green backdrop for perennials, used as living screens to block unwanted views, or attached to other structures (such as the side of a building) to give support to vines. *Asarina scandens*, sweet peas (*Lathyrus* spp.), bitter melon (*Momordica charantia*), all types of *Clematis*, and *Dicentra scandens* are all great choices for trellises.

Climbing vines that attach themselves to structures by means of tendrils or curved petioles generally require slim supports that are easy for the vines to clasp. For these, I often use trellises made of wire mesh attached to posts. The wire becomes barely visible once the vine begins to grow, and even the most delicate vines find the mesh easy to climb on. Woven wire fencing, which comes in several heights, is sold by the roll and lasts many seasons. I buy it at a local farm-supply store, but it's also available at garden centers. Avoid using chicken wire, which rusts and weakens in just a few years.

CLINGERS COVER SOLID STRUCTURES

Clingers like ivy (*Hedera* spp.), Virginia creeper (*Parthenocissus quinquefolia*), and climbing hydrangea (*Hydrangea anomala* spp. *petiolaris*) look wonderful across solid fences, stone walls, and wooden garden screens. They look equally lovely bedecking buildings, but a warning before you swath your home in perennial clingers: wooden walls become impossible to paint and may rot from the moist environment created by clinging vines. Also, brickwork and stonework can eventually be damaged from rootlets that work their

Whether used as screens or to support vines on buildings, trellises work well in both formal and informal designs.

way into cracks and fissures in the surrounding mortar. Stucco walls are not safe either if there are any cracks in them.

Instead of tempting fate, I erect a wire trellis a foot or two from the house to allow air between the vine and the wall. This way, I can have the look of vines growing next to my house without worrying about the walls becoming permanently scarred.

ARCHES SUPPORT ALL TYPES OF VINES

An open archway invites you not only to appreciate the vines growing upon it but also to pass through it. However, don't take your visitors on an entrancing trip to the garbage cans; make sure your arch opens onto a gorgeous garden scene. Two of the easiest places to incorporate an arch are at the front sidewalk leading to your house, and in line with a fence or hedge that divides your yard into separate garden rooms.

I consider 4 feet wide the minimum opening for an arch. A vine needs at least this much space to grow on an arch and still allow easy passage through it. And don't neglect to plant your arches wisely. Vines with dangerously sharp thorns on a narrow arch will have visitors to your garden fearing for their safety.

An arch can also be used as a focal point in the back of a garden bed, perhaps covered by prized climbing roses. At the end of a path, an open archway can invite strollers into an undiscovered garden room. An arch with a bench beneath it becomes a perfect spot to sit and admire your garden handiwork.

Arches are versatile structures to grow vines on. Clingers, climbers, twiners, and scramblers are all at home on them. Clematis, roses, *Kadsura japonica*, and black-eyed Susan vine (*Thunbergia alata*) are just a few of my favorites for arches.

Position simple wrought-iron archways to mark the boundaries between garden rooms.

A sturdy arch ably frames an entryway and provides a sense of enclosure.

Open roofing allows dappled sunlight through to the pathway.

A wood trellis provides additional support for twining vines.

Strong supports withstand the substantial weight of heavy vines.

Underplantings add interest from the ground up.

ARBORS AND PERGOLAS CREATE COMFORTABLE SHADE

Although the terms arbor and pergola have become interchangeable in modern American gardening circles, they were originally very different structures. In Roman times, an arbor was a wooden structure onto which vines were trained to provide a comfortable place out of the sun for sitting. Grapes were often grown on these structures, which further encouraged visitors to linger. Pergolas, Italian for "projecting roof," performed a much different function. They provided shelter over walkways, and if planted with fragrant and beautiful flowering vines, they created a satisfying stroll for garden lovers. The word pergola also referred to parallel rows of trees planted to form a protective canopy overhead. However you define them, they make great structures to grow vines on.

Arbors and pergolas have vertical supports, walls that are either enclosed with lath panels or left open, and a roof. The roofs are not solid, but have an open cross-bracing that allows vines to climb up the support posts and then across, creating dappled shade. These structures are larger than arches and vary in shape and design.

A patio that bakes in summer could be made more welcoming with the addition of a wisteria-covered arbor. Nonfruiting vines are best for growing on these structures, as fallen fruit is messy, slippery, and attractive to wasps and flies. I recommend using vines that shed their leaves in fall and let the winter sun through; a patio overhung with evergreen vines could prove a dank and chilly environment for sun-starved gardeners.

Substantial vines like trumpet creeper (*Campsis radicans*), cross vine (*Bignonia capreolata* 'Tangerine Beauty'), climbing roses like *Rosa* 'New Dawn', fiveleaf akebia (*Akebia*

A Selection of Great Climbers

ANNUALS

Asarina scandens 'Mystic Pink'

Hyacinth bean – *Dipogon lablab*

Old-fashioned morning glory – *Ipomoea × purpurea*

Cardinal climber – *Ipomoea quamoclit*

PERENNIALS

Carolina jessamine – *Gelsemium sempervirens*

Lonicera periclymenum 'Belgica'

Native honeysuckle –*Lonicera sempervirens*

Muscadine grapes –'Sweet Jenny', 'Watergate' (golden), and 'Ison' (purple)

Virginia creeper – *Parthenocissus quiquefolia*

Rosa 'New Dawn'

Schizophragma 'Brookside Littleleaf'

Thunbergia battescombei

Pyramidal structures like obelisks add architectural interest. They look good either alone or placed in containers.

The elegance of wrought iron is equally at home in formal and informal beds alike.

Match Your Structures to Your Site

Before building or buying ornamental structures to grow your vines on, consider the materials used to build your house and outbuildings, and the materials used for paving driveways and walks. Repeating these materials in garden-project construction is a simple way to visually unify your house and garden. Careful consideration may also reveal that certain materials would not produce satisfying results in your particular site. For example, my old wooden farmhouse would look silly juxtaposed with a brick and wrought-iron pergola, while a formal brick home with brick sidewalks practically begs for one.

Also, try to incorporate elements of the architectural design of your dwelling into your vine supports. A low-slung brick ranch might look best with a complementary wide and flat pergola, while the curved palladium windows of a modern two-story could be repeated with elegant metal arches. If you have an intriguing roofline, copy it on a smaller scale for an arbor. The design of your fence, if attractive, could be copied when building trellises.

Simple cedar posts make sturdy vine supports for twining vines like morning glories and purple hyacinth beans in the author's garden.

quinata), and grape vines (*Vitis* spp.) all lend themselves well to growing on pergolas and arbors, as these structures are expected to carry the heavy weight of cross-bracing and vine mass.

These large structures are visually dominant in a garden or landscape, so select vines that shine in all seasons. Beware of plants that are borderline hardy in your climate and may require severe pruning after harsh winters. Also avoid those that suffer afflictions in your climate, like rust or powdery mildew, which could make your pergola an eyesore rather than an attraction.

OBELISKS AND TUTEURS CAN BE FORMAL OR INFORMAL

Smaller structures like obelisks and tuteurs—from the French word meaning to train—are perfect for growing vines in containers or for tucking vines into tightly planted beds and borders. I've seen both of these structures made from metal and wood, but the prettiest one that I've seen was made of wrought iron.

These rounded, or in the case of obelisks, pyramidal, structures range from 2 to 8 feet tall and 6 to 20 inches wide. Taller models can add vertical accents to tiny gardens in place of larger, space-hungry plants. Their formal lines work well flanking an entryway or lining a patio to create summer privacy. But don't be put off by their formal, elegant style if your garden is informal in design, for a single tuteur or obelisk covered by an exuberant morning glory or night-blooming moonvine will not look out of place.

CLIMBERS ABLY SCALE POSTS

The simplest vine support is a sturdy post anchored solidly in the ground. I use cedar posts cut from dead *Juniperus virginiana* to grow vines on because they look appropriately rustic in my sunny pasture garden. These 8-foot-tall posts work great for vigorous twiners like purple hyacinth beans (*Lablab purpureus*) and my collection of morning glories (*Ipomoea* spp.).

For some heavy twiners like honeysuckle (*Lonicera* spp.), I wrap posts in heavy wire fencing to keep the plant from sliding down into a messy heap as it gains in mass. The fencing is none too attractive at first but it's disguised by season's end.

FENCES PROVIDE STURDY SURFACES FOR VINES

Gardeners who love open views can use split-rail fences to loosely frame their garden pictures. The widely spaced, rustic-looking, wooden rails create enclosure without actually keeping anything in or out. It would then be a shame to clutter a split-rail fence's delicate visual brushstrokes with masses of thick vines. This is why trailing rose canes look so attractive and are so often used to adorn split rail and other types of open, airy fences. And it's much easier to weave a thorny cane between a fence's rails than to try to tack the rose to a trellis.

If your tastes turn more to wrought iron than split rail, consider dressing your fence in slow-growing, evergreen vines. The formal look of wrought iron calls for vines that are neat and precise in outline. The most beautiful example that I've seen used is Carolina jessamine (*Gelsemium sempervirens*), with its deep-green, glossy foliage and fragrant yellow flowers. Variegated ivies of delicate leaf and slow growth provide excellent coverage also. Two good choices are the green and gold *Hedera helix* 'Goldheart' and the marbled gray, green, and white *H. helix* 'Glacier'.

Solid fences soften in appearance when they are graced by the leafy presence of vines. A friend of mine enclosed her front garden in an attractive picket fence that supports numerous climbers. The 3-inch-wide, flat pickets are hard for many plants to grasp at first, but with a helping hand to get them started, the vines eventually get the idea. Swathed in sweet autumn clematis (*Clematis terniflora*), as well as annuals like the scarlet-red cardinal climber (*Ipomoea* × *multifida*), the fence is an outstanding feature of her garden.

Cloaked in colorful coverings, vine supports add structural interest to your garden while linking it firmly to the surrounding architecture. Be adventuresome in your use of these beautiful structures and your outdoor paradise will take on a whole new look. In gardening, sometimes the sky really is the limit.

Trailing vines ably grace fences of all types. These ornery rose canes are easily and elegantly tamed by letting them meander through fence posts and railings.

FRANCES WENNER

has been gardening in the Kansas City area for more than 25 years. She writes for a local garden bulletin and lectures regularly for several horticultural organizations.

Build a Rustic
Garden Arbor

The beauty and utility of this unpretentious arbor provide backyard privacy and planting opportunities galore. The author swathed posts and trelliswork with her favorite climbers.

VINE FEVER caught me early. My garden dreams were draped and swagged in clematis, rose, and honeysuckle. Out in the garden, I crammed vines onto every inch of fence and over every available structure, whether shrub, picket, or trellis. Still, it was clear that the extravagant roses and muscular wisteria I craved would overwhelm any ordinary garden structure. These thoughts continued to bubble along in my subconscious until a trip to England provided an unexpected piece of inspiration.

While visiting the charming garden adjacent to a small Somerset nursery, I was struck by the beauty and utility of a simple wooden arbor through which the garden path passed. Its rustic good looks seemed to complement the whole garden, and the billowing roses and tangle of porcelain berry appeared sublimely content. Happily,

Materials List

CCA-treated lumber was used for all of the arbor components. Posts should be treated since they will be sunk into the ground, but cedar or redwood are good alternatives.

- 14: 10-ft.-long 4x4 posts
- 36: 8-ft.-long 2x4 boards for horizontal supports, facings, and trelliswork on the arbor back
- 2: 11-ft.-long 2x4 boards for the trelliswork on the end posts
- 19: 13-ft.-long 2x6 crossbeams
- 38: 2x2 vertical braces—24 cut to 7$\frac{1}{2}$-inch lengths, 14 cut to 10-inch lengths
- 46: 1x2 slats for trelliswork in varying lengths between 5 ft. and 6 ft.
- 8d and 4d nails for tacking boards into place
- Lag screws and #8 Phillips head screws

Once a location for the arbor was picked, the ground was tilled before beginning construction. This alleviated the hassle of digging around the posts.

With the help of a rented power auger, the posts were set in holes 2 feet deep. A post-hole digger would also get the job done, albeit more slowly.

Bruce, my spouse and chief garden engineer, was with me and took pictures of the structure, including the construction details.

BUILDING THE ARBOR BECOMES A FAMILY PROJECT

Once home, we saw that the obvious place to build our own arbor was along the east boundary of our property. There it would close the circle of our backyard privacy. The spot is unusual in that it occupies slightly sloping ground. Books advised us that the arbor location needed to be level, but since level does not exist on our two acres, we decided to position the arbor where we thought it would look at home and hoped for the best.

We took careful measurements, purchased lumber and hardware, and rented a gas-powered post-hole digger. We decided to use CCA-treated lumber for the arbor because of its weather resistance. Cedar or redwood would have been good looking and durable enough, but also considerably more expensive. (CCA-treated lumber should not be used near vegetables because chemicals from the lumber can leach into the soil.)

Before beginning construction, we tilled the area we planned to plant. Doing so meant we could till everything without the hassle of working around the posts, which would have required a lot of hand digging. Next we dug 14 holes for the 10-foot 4x4 posts in two rows of seven, to a depth of 2 feet. We used the rented power auger to save time and effort, but a muscle-powered post-hole digger would have done the job. We set the posts in two parallel rows, 11 feet apart. And we measured as we went to make sure the top of each post was precisely 8 feet aboveground; this made the arbor follow the contour of the land.

Arbor Details

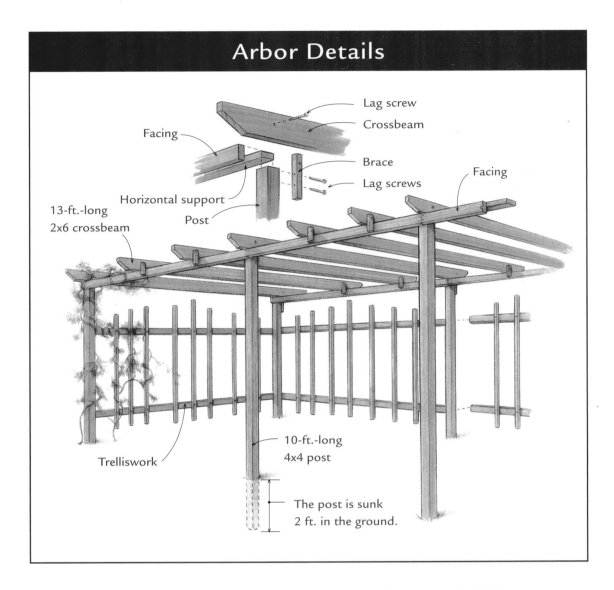

Lag screw

Crossbeam

Facing

Brace

Lag screws

Facing

Horizontal support

Post

13-ft.-long
2x6 crossbeam

Trelliswork

10-ft.-long
4x4 post

The post is sunk
2 ft. in the ground.

The posts were spaced 8 feet apart on center, and topped with 8-foot-long 2x4 horizontal supports. The supports were laid wide side down, meeting in the center of the tops of the posts. We tacked the supports with 8d nails to hold them in place, and then added the facings. The facings were also 8-foot 2x4s, one board for each horizontal support, placed flush with the top outside edge of the horizontal support. Once all of the supports and facings were tacked on, we secured them by drilling and setting 2½-inch-long, ¼-inch hex-head lag screws. The screws for the horizontal supports were countersunk because the crossbeams were placed directly on top of them.

CROSSBEAMS CREATE A SENSE OF ENCLOSURE

A total of 19 crossbeams span the top of the arbor. They are 13-foot lengths of 2x6 boards, with both ends partially beveled at 45-degree angles. One beam is situated over each pair of posts, and in each interval between the posts, two more beams are equally spaced. To secure the crossbeams, we mounted vertical 2x2 braces, cut to 10-inch lengths, onto the back side of each post. More braces, 2x2s cut to 7½-inch lengths, were added to the front of the facing for the beams running in between the posts.

The braces were positioned, their bottoms flush with the bottom of the facing, and then

The author's husband and son built the arbor over a few weeks' time. Here, they join the posts together with horizontal supports.

Prior to planting, the soil was amended with compost. Then, at the base of each post, a good-sized hole was dug for a carefully chosen rose or clematis.

fastened with two 2½-inch-long, ¼-inch lag screws. Then we placed the crossbeams against the braces, securing them with two 2½-inch screws through each brace and into the beam. The beams between the posts were secured further with 3½-inch lag screws, driven through the horizontal supports and up into the beam.

The final step was to close off the back and bottom end of the arbor with trelliswork. We attached two rows of 8-foot 2x4 horizontal boards to the back of the posts, spaced 40 inches apart, and fastened each with two 2½-inch lag screws on each end. Then we added vertical 1x2 slats to form the trelliswork. The arbor was completed—an empty canvas to paint with my favorite plants!

SWATHING THE ARBOR IN VINES

While my husband and son worked on the arbor, I prepared beds at the foot of the posts and along the full length of the arbor's back. I amended the soil with as much organic matter as I could lay my hands on, and dug a deep hole at the base of each post for a rose. On the back side of the posts, another hole was dug for clematis. These two plants would form the backbone of my composition.

Now came the challenge of choosing from among the hundreds of roses and dozens of clematis available. Among roses, 'Dr. W. Van Fleet', with its luxuriant, baby-pink bushels of bloom, took pride of place. The Dr.'s offspring, 'New Dawn', and cousin, 'White Dawn', were also added to bring their blossoms and shiny foliage to the shadier end of the arbor. 'Madame Isaac Pereire', raspberry-pink and heavenly scented, found a place of honor, and 'Sally Holmes', 'Louise Odier', and 'Penelope' added their special charms. 'Alchemyst', a longtime favorite grown elsewhere in the garden and cherished for its massive blooms of whirling peach, apricot, and cream, was a must, as were David Austin's 'Eden' and soft-yellow 'Graham Thomas'. Between the posts along the front of the arbor, I added shrub roses such as 'Bonica', 'The Fairy', and 'Gruss an Aachen'.

I chose clematis vines to complement the roses while in bloom and to add interest to the arbor later in the season. *Clematis* 'Jackmanii Superba' twines its deep-purple stars through the arms of 'Dr. W. Van Fleet', while sky blue 'Perle d'Azur' climbs the post at the arbor's entrance. *C. alpina* 'Frances Rivis' welcomes spring on one corner, while the huge, violet-blue flowers of 'Lasurstern' impress all who view their pointed, gently undulating sepals and creamy boss of stamens. 'Niobe' flashes its deep-ruby blooms and adds drama and richness, and 'Ville de Lyon' offers a textured, pink-velvet bloom with a unique, touchable look.

Many of the smaller clematis species bloom later in the season. *C. texensis* and its cultivars add interest with bell-shaped blooms opening to cupped stars. 'Duchess of Albany' is a strong grower with true pink flowers, while 'Sir Trevor Lawrence' adds a veil of bright-red bells. The C. *viticella* cultivars are equally delightful with tiny, dangling bells in shades of purple and violet. 'Etoile Violette' proclaims its violet color boldly, while 'Royal Velours' is the darkest purple of all. The species itself, C. *viticella*, has a certain grace that its cultivars often lack. Its flowers are smaller, but they are held on stiff horizontal stems while the tiny violet bells shimmer and sway in the breeze. Enchanting!

A PLACE TO ENJOY THE VIEW AND LUXURIATE IN THE ROSES

In the center of the arbor, we placed a cedar bench of simple design to blend with the structure and provide a place of repose among the roses. Flanking the bench, two terra-cotta pots were set on brick platforms and hold long-blooming sun-lovers like petunias, trailing ivies, and licorice plant (*Helichrysum petiolare*) for summer-long interest. From this spot, we enjoy a cross view of our garden, softly framed by the rose and vine-clad arbor. The beds beneath the posts are filled with an ever changing array of bulbs, annuals, and perennials as I search for the best choices to set off the arbor climbers. Lavender and catmint seem natural with roses, and three varieties of honeysuckle twine upwards, blooming all summer and growing bushier and more fragrant each season. The pale-yellow, deliciously scented 'Graham Thomas' honeysuckle (*Lonicera periclymenum* 'Graham Thomas') twines over the trellis behind the bench, pouring its perfume over the fortunate who pause to rest.

The arbor has become one of our garden's loveliest and most appreciated features. A neighbor watching the construction inquired, "Going to have a grape arbor?" Having watched us fill the garden with myriad varieties of trees, shrubs, and perennials for nearly 20 years, he should have known better!

A simple cedar bench is situated in the middle of the arbor. Those who have time to stop and rest can enjoy a view across the garden and the delicious scent of 'Graham Thomas' honeysuckle.

LYNN HUNT

is a consulting rosarian
and an accredited horti-
cultural judge for the
American Rose Society.
She gardens in Woolford,
Maryland.

Lift
Climbing Roses
to New Heights

Climbing roses need
sturdy structures for
support; otherwise,
they will topple over
under their own
weight. Arbors, gaze-
bos, and tripodlike
structures all work well.

I T'S HARD TO IMAGINE a more idyllic picture
than a country cottage covered in climbing roses.
Whether arching over a doorway, smothering a
brick wall, twining around a rustic pole, or reaching
up into the branches of an old tree, climbing roses
are the show-stoppers of the garden. They lend a sense of
maturity to any setting. They can soften the most formal
architecture. And their ability to add instant height can
bring a ho-hum area of the garden to life in short order.

CLIMBING ROSES ARE RECENT

Despite their centuries-old appearance, climbers are
Johnny-come-latelys in the rose world. Hybrid descen-
dants of ancient wild climbers became stylish in the late
1800s. Many large-flowered climbers appeared as a result
of sports from existing bushes. One group of climbers
was born in 1802 when a Charleston rice farmer planted

the seed of a chance cross between the China rose 'Old Blush' and *R. moschata*, the musk rose. Seeds from that rose, 'Champney's Pink Cluster', produced the first reblooming climbers. A French nurseryman living in Charleston sent promising seedlings to his brother in Paris. These roses, known as Noisettes, became famous for their ability to bloom repeatedly and "climb."

Of course, climbing roses can't really climb at all. In fact, they should probably be described as leaners. Their long canes don't possess the tendrils that true climbing plants like vines and clematis use to cling to objects. Climbing roses need help, no matter what structure they are tied to.

CLIMBERS ADORN WALLS

Most gardeners get their start with climbing roses by training them to frame an entrance-way or adorn a trellis next to the house. The first rule for success is to make sure your rose structure is weather resistant and rugged. The beams supporting a front porch will probably last for ages, but a flimsy, cheap trellis might not make it through the first season. Also, keep in mind that whenever you plant close to a house or a garage, the ground there is likely to be the driest in the garden. Dig your hole at least 18 inches from the foundation and prepare the soil with plenty of organic matter. Maintain a generous watering schedule for at least the first year, and be patient—most climbers will take three years to hit peak performance.

Aside from trellises, there are several ways to train a rose up an exterior wall. In England, where many houses are built of stone, gardeners drive or drill eyelets into the mortar every 18 inches, then string 12-gauge galvanized steel wire horizontally between the eyelets. The wire is stretched as tightly as possible, then the canes are tied to the support with thick twine. This method also works with brick walls. Another approach is to string wire from eyelets beneath your eaves to wooden stakes in the ground with the thought of creating a kind of wire fan.

Climbing Roses with Lofty Reputations

Here are some popular Climbers and Ramblers that have proven to be dependable performers across the United States. Most are highly rated by the American Rose Society.

NAME	HEIGHT (FT.)	FLOWER COLOR
Climbing Roses		
'Altissimo'	8-10	medium red
'America'	10+	orange pink
'Compassion'	8-12	orange pink
'Dublin Bay'	8-10	medium red
'Fourth of July'	8	red blend
'Handel'	12	red blend
'Cl. Iceberg'	12+	white
'Pierre de Ronsard'	15	pink blend
'Royal Sunset'	8-12	apricot blend
'Sombreuil'	10-14	creamy white
'Cl. Souvenir de la Malmaison'	12	light pink
Ramblers		
'American Pillar'	12-20	pink/white
'Paul's Himalayan Musk Rambler'	20+	pink
'Veilchenblau'	12-14	mauve
Miniature Climbers		
'Jeanne Lajoie'	6-7	pink
'Cl. Rainbow's End'	6-8	yellow blend
David Austin Roses		
'Graham Thomas'	10-12	yellow
'A Shropshire Lad'	8	apricot blend
'Snow Goose'	10	white

Paint structures colors to compliment your Climbing and Rambling roses.

For something less formal, try growing climbers up a tree or post. It's a great way to add a splash of color to a drab area.

Climbers like 'New Dawn' and 'Pierre de Ronsard' (also known as 'Eden') make a stunning statement trained this way on either side of a front door.

CREATE GARDEN STANDOUTS

Away from the house, your choice of structures for climbing roses is limited only by your imagination. It's been said that dotting the landscape with climbers is like hanging beautiful paintings in strategic locations—with a bit of planning and an artistic eye, you can create signature accents in your garden. Arbors, whether rustic willow, elaborate latticework, or functional copper pipe, can be the focal point of the garden when embellished by a rose such as 'Cl. Cécile Brünner'. The sight of 'Souvenir de la Malmaison' forming an awning of blooms over a pergola is one few works of art could rival.

In my garden, I've fashioned my own mural with freestanding trellis panels that create a living wall of blooms and a natural pathway between my house and the house next door. By mixing *Clematis*, passion flower (*Passiflora* spp.), and other climbing vines in with the roses, I can enjoy privacy as well as a parade of colorful flowers that lasts all season.

CLIMBERS FLOURISH WHEN ALLOWED TO GROW LATERALLY

Fences and roses make beautiful companions. 'Blaze Improved' or 'Joseph's Coat' can stop traffic when trained along a picket fence. The blooms of 'Sombreuil' and 'Cl. Iceberg' are unforgettable cascading over a rustic wooden fence. Ramblers, with their long, supple canes and dense clusters of small flowers, generally bloom only once a year, but will put on a spectacular 20-foot-long show. I like twine, tie tape, or cut-up old pantyhose to secure the rose canes to the fences.

For a European flair, twine a rose like 'Altissimo' around a pillar. Or create a catenary, which is a garland of blooms wrapped around ropes strung between two uprights. Or try growing a rose up into a tree. I am hitching the Bourbon rose 'Zéphirine Drouhin' with loose string to a nearby cedar tree. This nearly thornless rose isn't fussy about a little shade or less-than-ideal soil conditions.

Need more ideas? Let hardy 'Sea Foam' scramble over a stump. Train the miniature

"The first rule for success is to make sure your rose structure is weather resistant and rugged."

climber 'Jeanne La Joie' up a tripod as an accent in the garden border. Or use 'Compassion' to screen out an eyesore. Whether you end up with a cottage festooned with climbers or a single pillar, you'll find these roses do much more than elevate your garden's vista. They also lift your spirit.

Fences and roses make wonderful companions. As with other structures, you'll need to secure the rose canes to the fence for support. Twine and tie-tape work best. Plastic-coated wire and nylon string can dig into stems.

JOE TADDIA

has been restoring Colonial and Victorian homes for 40 years. He is currently restoring the old Scoville Tavern in Watertown, Connecticut.

Handcrafting a Sturdy Arbor

Easy to build, both sides of this arbor take less than a day to assemble. Cut out the top pieces, and you're ready to put it in place.

I'VE ALWAYS LIKED building garden structures, but my business usually keeps me elbow deep in the restoration of Colonial and Victorian houses. So when a client with a big idea and a tiny budget wanted me to create an eye-catching arbor for her yard, I jumped at the chance. I think an arbor makes an artful addition to any garden. Its tracery lends sculptural elegance to stark, wintry landscapes, and when covered by flowering vines in summer, an arbor becomes an enticing bower—a place to linger and visit with a friend or to rest in cooling shade.

We ended up building the arbor around a fence and gate, but the simple, rustic design I came up with will fit into many settings. By making it a little larger, you could transform the arbor into a small pergola that would look great placed at the end of a walkway. Put a bench inside, cover the arbor with wisteria, and you've got a cozy sitting spot. If you wanted to add the arbor to a child's play area, you could outfit it with a swing.

You should be able to do everything in a single weekend. All it takes are basic carpentry skills, a few pieces of standard lumber, and a toolbox equipped with the basics. The most sophisticated power tool you'll need is a circular saw.

THE MATERIALS
ARE READILY AVAILABLE

To keep the project affordable, I used inexpensive pine and Douglas fir for everything except the vertical pieces that will be partially buried in the ground. For these, I used pressure-treated wood that lasts for years before it begins to rot. As an alternative, you could waterproof the upright parts with a preservative. For a more attractive look, you could build the entire arbor of cedar or redwood. Cedar construction boosts the cost for materials from about $75 up to about $250; redwood would be even more expensive. You should be able to get the rest of the materials—carriage bolts, nuts, and washers, as well as some sand and gravel—at a local lumberyard. To help prevent moisture damage to the finished arbor, use galvanized nails; they won't rust and stain the wood. You can finish the arbor with paint or stain if you wish, but I think it looks good and requires less maintenance if simply left to weather.

Whichever type of wood you use, plan on spending the better part of a day building the

A simple arbor provides support for sweet autumn clematis (*Clematis temiflora*). The structure's unfinished wood will weather to a silvery gray to better complement the golden spires of *Ligularia stenocephala* 'The Rocket'.

arbor, and figure on another half day to dig the holes and put the structure into place. You'll need a toolbox equipped with a circular saw, an electric or cordless drill and a ⅜-inch bit that can drill a hole at least 7 inches deep, a spade or post-hole digger, a combination square, a tape measure, a chisel, a hammer, a carpenter's level, and a wrench.

BUILD THE TOP OF THE ARBOR FIRST

Start the project by cutting the cross braces, the two pieces that span the top of the arbor. The first step is cutting the lower corners off two 6-foot 2x6 boards as shown. This is just a decorative touch, so to refine the design, you could make more intricate, curved cuts. You can speed the process by marking and making the first cut, then using the scrap piece as a template for marking the other cuts.

Once the ends have been trimmed, clamp the two cross braces together, and place them bottom side up to mark the position for each

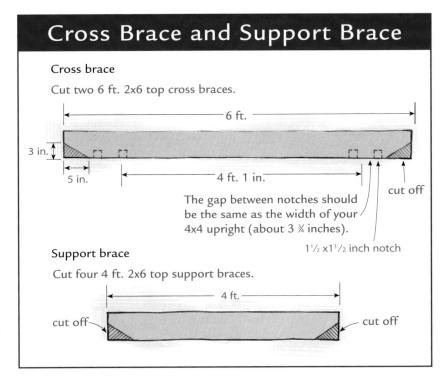

Cross Brace and Support Brace

Cross brace

Cut two 6 ft. 2x6 top cross braces.

6 ft.

3 in.

5 in.　　4 ft. 1 in.

cut off

The gap between notches should be the same as the width of your 4x4 upright (about 3 ¾ inches).

1½ x1½ inch notch

Support brace

Cut four 4 ft. 2x6 top support braces.

4 ft.

cut off　　cut off

Notch the support braces by measuring the width of the notches with a piece of scrap 2x6 (use the 2-inch side).

Decorative cuts add style to the finished arbor. Use a saw to trim triangular pieces off the ends of the support and cross braces.

Cut the outer edges of each notch with a circular saw set to cut at 1½ inches. Use the saw to make repeated passes between the cuts.

Trim away the waste with a chisel.

of the four notches that get cut in each board. Each pair of notches should be the width of a 2x4 apart. To get the precise distance, lay a piece of 2x4, wide side down, across the cross brace. Use a combination square to get a good right angle.

After marking the notches, set the circular saw to cut 1½ inches deep, and cut each side of the notch first. Then make repeated passes between the two outer cuts, cutting away a little more of the wood each time. Use a chisel to clear any remaining wood from the notches.

T-SHAPED SUPPORTS PROVIDE A SOLID FOUNDATION

To make the T-shaped supports that provide the arbor's strength, secure a pair of 2x6s to the top of each of the 4x4 support posts. In the finished assembly, the support braces are parallel to each other and perfectly aligned.

Start by making decorative cuts, like those at the end of the cross brace, on what will be the lower corners of the four 4-foot 2x6 support braces. Use one of the pieces left over from the cross braces to mark the corners for cutting. Look for knots or unsightly imperfections in the wood—this is the time to decide which side of the wood should show on the outside of the arbor.

Once the support braces are cut, attach them to the 4x4 support posts. To do this, lay one of the support posts on its side, and put one of the support braces across the post centered and flush to the top. Use two 10d galvanized nails to tack the brace in place. Carefully turn the assembly over, and fasten a second 2x6 so that it aligns with the one you just fastened. Tack the second piece in place. Carefully drill two ⅜-inch holes

Drill two holes through the support braces. Insert carriage bolts, and finish by tightening each one with a nut.

Make T-shape supports by aligning two support braces with the top of a 4x4 pressure-treated post. Center the pieces, and make sure they are at a right angle to the 4x4. Tack them in place.

through the 2x6s and the 4x4 post. Avoid drilling into the tacking nails. Then tap the carriage bolts through the holes and secure with a washer and nut.

GETTING A LATTICE-LIKE LOOK ON THE SIDES

Now you're ready to complete the lattice-like sides of the arbor. Slip an 8-foot 2x4 between the support braces on each side of the 4x4 post. Position these side rails so they are parallel to the 4x4 post and 12 inches away from it. Fasten at the top with 10d nails. Run a tape measure down the 4x4, and place the first ladder rail 12 inches from the support brace; the second should be positioned 24 inches down, the third 42 inches down, and the fourth 60 inches down. Then center the 1x2 ladder rails on the 4x4 (they should extend about ¾ inch beyond the side rails on each side). Fasten them with a 6d galvanized nail or two at each end and in the middle.

An Arbor Builder's Shopping List

To build an arbor 7½ feet tall and 6 feet wide (outside edge to outside edge), you'll need the following materials. To build a wider arbor that is more like a pergola, buy longer pieces for the cross braces.

LUMBER	QUANTITY	LENGTH	SIZE
Support posts*	2	10 ft.	4 x 4
Top cross brace	2	6 ft.	2 x 6
Arbor support brace	4	4 ft.	2 x 6
Side rails	4	8 ft.	2 x 4
Ladder rails	8	32 in.	¾ in. x ½ in.
Stabilizer	2	4 ft.	2 x 4

(optional: see the illustration on p. 105)

Note: Pine is acceptable for all wood except support posts and side rails, which should be cedar, redwood, or pressure-treated.

HARDWARE AND MISCELLANEOUS

Carriage bolts	8	8 in.	⅜ in.
Washers	8		⅜ in.
Nuts	4		⅜ in.

1 lb. 6d galvanized common nails for securing ladder rails to the arbor.

1 lb. 10d galvanized common nails for fastening cross braces, side rails, and stabilizer bars. Also for positioning support braces.

Approx. 100 lb. each of sand and gravel.

Lay the two sides on the ground, and position the notched cross braces on them. Before you raise the arbor, check to make sure all the pieces fit together easily. You may have to trim the notches a little if the fit is too tight. It's a lot easier to make these little modifications on the ground than once the arbor is upright.

RAISE THE ARBOR INTO PLACE

To get the arbor in its final position, you'll need to dig six holes: two for the uprights and four to take the bottom of the side rails. For the support posts, dig two holes 36 inches deep and 48 inches apart on center. In other words, the distance from the center of one hole to the center of the other should be 4 feet. Pick a level patch of ground; not only will the arbor look odd if perched on a slope, but it will also be that much more difficult to position it properly. Once the holes are dug, place about 6 inches of gravel into the bottom of each. Then, on either side of the main holes, dig two small, 6-inch-deep holes to receive the bottoms of the side rails.

When you're ready to actually raise the arbor into place, an assistant might prove useful. Slide the support post of one side of the arbor into the deep center hole so that the stabilizer board rests on the ground. About 7½ feet of the upright should be aboveground. Use a level to make sure the post is plumb and the support braces are level. Then fill the hole with sand, packing it as you go. The post may shift a little as you fill in the hole, so check it a few times. It's easier to make minor adjustments as you go than it is to pull the whole assembly out of the ground and start over.

Slide the second side of the assembly into the other predug holes. Add some sand and gravel, but do not pack it.

Assemble the arbor on the ground to make sure all the pieces go together easily. The cross braces should fit snugly over the support braces; a good fit may require a little extra trimming. Then take the arbor apart so it can by erected upright, piece by piece.

When they are in place, nail on a stabilizing, 4-foot length of 2x4 about 6 inches above the bottom of the 2x4 side rails. Since these 2x4s are there to help support the arbor when you raise it into place, don't drive the 10d nails in all the way because you may want to remove the stabilizers once the arbor has been erected. But if you plan to build a swing in the arbor, leave the stabilizers; they'll add needed support. Once you're finished, assemble the second side of the arbor in the same way.

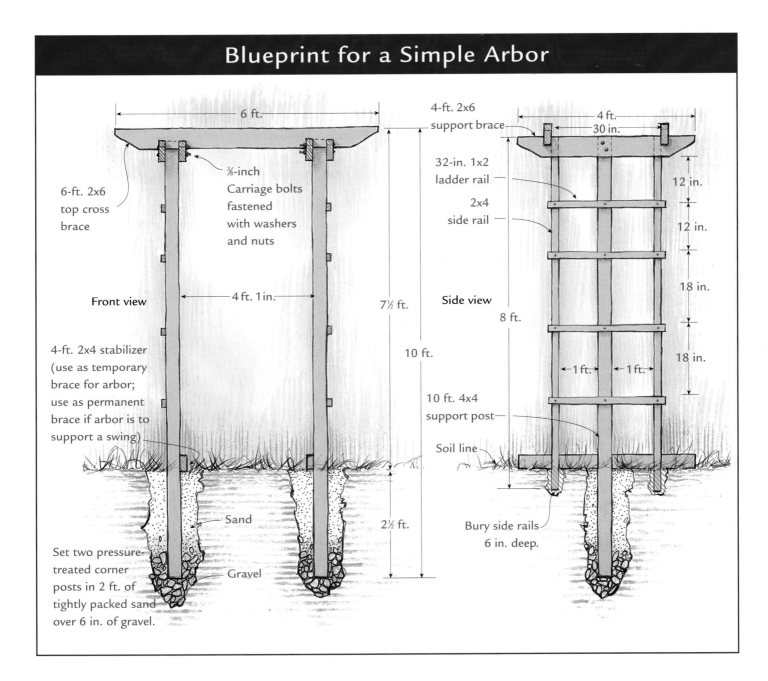

6 ft.

4-ft. 2x6 support brace

4 ft.

30 in.

⅜-inch Carriage bolts fastened with washers and nuts

6-ft. 2x6 top cross brace

32-in. 1x2 ladder rail

2x4 side rail

12 in.

12 in.

18 in.

Front view

4 ft. 1 in.

7½ ft.

Side view

8 ft.

4-ft. 2x4 stabilizer (use as temporary brace for arbor; use as permanent brace if arbor is to support a swing)

10 ft.

18 in.

1 ft.

1 ft.

10 ft. 4x4 support post

Soil line

Sand

2½ ft.

Bury side rails 6 in. deep.

Set two pressure-treated corner posts in 2 ft. of tightly packed sand over 6 in. of gravel.

Gravel

MAKE THE STRUCTURE PLUMB AND LEVEL

Standing on a ladder, cap the arbor with the two cross braces. Unless you're very lucky, very skillful, or both, the arbor is going to require some adjusting before it's all plumbed up and leveled. Use the secured side of the arbor as a fixed reference, and adjust the second side forward or back, left or right, or up or down, whatever is required to make the posts plumb and the cross braces and support braces level. When everything is lined up, fill the second hole with sand and gravel, packing it as you go. Check the structure with a level again. If it's true, nail the notched cross brace into position with 10d nails. If you want, you can remove the 2x4 leveler boards at the bottom of each side.

SYDNEY EDDISON

is a long-time contributor to *Fine Gardening*. She is the author of numerous gardening books, including *The Self-Taught Gardener*.

Build a Sapling Trellis

This trellis, made from saplings gathered with a lopper in the woods, screens a dog run and adds an upright accent to the terrace.

I WAS INSPIRED to make a sapling trellis when I saw tepees of cedar poles cleverly devised by Peter Wooster and Gary Keim. The tepees provided perpendicular accents on a level site. A variety of wonderful annual vines scaled these supports and made me think I could do something similar.

My southwestern Connecticut perennial garden has a shrub-and-tree-covered hillside as a vertical backdrop, but I wanted something tall and upright on the terrace.

My first structure was a scaled-down copy of the Wooster-Keim model. I cut down three maple saplings from the understory of our woodlot and installed them—equidistant from each other—in a half whiskey barrel filled with soil. I lashed together the tops of the saplings with natural raffia. You could use twine, but I like raffia because it gives a little and it's possible to fashion a very tight joint. The tepee was about 5 feet tall. I planted a delicate morning-glory relative, star glory (*Ipomoea*

Maple saplings culled from the
forest are lashed together with
raffia or twine. Half whiskey barrels
support the structure.

See details of lashing
trellis joints on p. 110.

quamoclit), around the saplings, and soon the seedlings coiled up the supports and wove a tent of lacy foliage and scarlet blossoms. I was delighted with the effect, and the price was right—the cost of some raffia and a half whiskey barrel.

EXPERIMENTING WITH MATERIALS

The next year, my trellis-making was more ambitious. The idea of making an arch to screen the dog run from the terrace intrigued me. Again, half whiskey barrels, one on either side of the opening into the run, provided anchorage for the maple saplings. Plastic pots of a comparable size would work equally well, but I don't recommend clay pots, which are breakable.

I made two single arches, held apart with cross members, like the rungs in a ladder. Matching the two arches proved difficult, and the result was slightly lopsided and asymmetrical. The different sizes and varying grains of the saplings made it hard to bend them in perfectly parallel arches. But eventually, the large, heart-shaped leaves of moonflower (*Ipomoea alba*) and morning glory (*I. tricolor*) vines hid any imperfections.

I learned another lesson that summer—not to combine two vines of different growth habit on the same trellis. Moonflower is a gorgeous but rampageous grower. It wins hands-down in the foliage contest, providing almost instant coverage and remaining hand-

"I like raffia (lashing) because it gives a little..."

A Few Good Annual Vines

Vines with climbing stems are particularly suitable for sapling structures. There are numerous annual vines that would be fun to try, including:

- Black-eyed Susan vine (*Thunbergia alata*)
- Cypress vine (*Ipomoea quamoclit*)
- Moonflower (*Ipomoea alba*)
- Morning glory (*Ipomoea tricolor*)
- Scarlet runner bean (*Phaseolus coccineus*)
- Potato vine (*Solanum jasminoides*)

Even in winter, a sapling trellis adds an interesting vertical element to the landscape.

Lashing Trellis Joints

Use finish nails to tack saplings together. The nails should be long enough to go all the way through the first sapling and into the middle of the second sapling. To tie off a crosspiece:

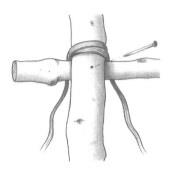

1 Wrap raffia (or twine) twice around the upright.

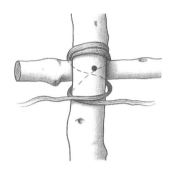

2 Cross raffia behind the upright.

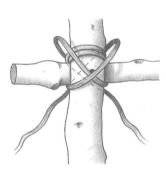

3 Cross raffia in front of the upright, and then cross behind the upright again.

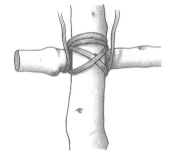

4 Wrap each end of the raffia up around the front of the crosspiece.

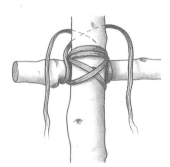

5 Cross ends behind upright and wrap down around crosspieces.

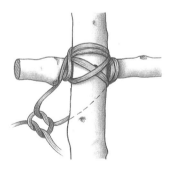

6 Pull raffia tight, and tie with a square knot.

some all summer, but it quickly swamped the less vigorous morning glory. While nothing is bluer or more heavenly than a 'Heavenly Blue' morning glory, its foliage looks shabby by the end of the season.

DESIGNING THE PERFECT TRELLIS

The most successful trellis I have made so far is 6½ feet tall and about 1 foot deep with a 5-foot-wide opening and a flat top. I made the trellis from saplings about 12 feet long and about 1½ inches in diameter at the base, culled from our woods with loppers. There are hundreds of saplings struggling for light beneath the dense canopy overhead, and most are tall, straight, and ideal for my purposes.

The size and design of the trellis can be infinitely varied. A deep trellis with long rungs could serve as a shady alcove for a bench. Or you could make a decorative screen by driving a series of uprights into the ground and making a sun-burst pattern by lashing on diagonal pieces. If you have a plentiful source of saplings, or enjoy sketching potential designs, experiment to your heart's content.

Supply List

1½-inch-diameter saplings

2 half whiskey barrels or similar planters

Raffia or twine

A few #4 or #6 finish nails (without heads), depending on thickness of saplings

Loppers for cutting heavy ends of saplings

Clippers for taking off any small twigs

Hammer

DONNA FREEMAN

gardens in Lake Oswego, Oregon. Her roses now lean gracefully against copper pipe trellises and arbors.

Build a Copper Pipe Trellis

I APPRECIATE THE cool shade of the towering fir trees in my suburban Portland garden, but my flowers don't. The roses sprawl toward the east in search of morning sun, and the delphiniums lean longingly toward the light. To support my wandering climbers, I wanted a trellis that would be decorative in summer and winter. I searched without success through catalogs and nurseries for carefree, long-lasting structures until, finally, I saw what I wanted in a local garden—a simple, but handsome, freestanding, copper trellis.

Copper appealed to me because it is so decorative. After a season in the elements, its bright color weathers to a deep, warm brown that blends nicely into the garden. As the years pass, oxidation slowly burnishes the brown to a soft, muted green.

An elegant support for a sprawling rose, this copper trellis looks better with each passing year.

Putting the Pieces Together

You can purchase all of the tools and supplies for making a copper pipe trellis at most plumbing- and home-supply stores. To make transporting the lengths of pipe easier, ask store personnel to cut them into lengths that fit easily into your car.

TOOLS

- Nylon or metal scouring pad
- Latex or rubber gloves
- Safety glasses
- Pipe cutter
- Brass propane torch
- Propane cylinder
- Flux brush
- Measuring tape

SUPPLIES

- Lead-free soldering wire
- Soldering flux
- Copper pipe:
  - four $3/4$-in. x 24-in. lengths of rigid copper pipe for the bottom vertical pieces
  - four $3/4$-in. x 18-in. lengths of rigid copper pipe for the horizontal crossbars
  - four $3/4$-in. x 12-in. lengths of rigid copper pipe for the upper vertical pieces
  - eight $1/2$-in. x 3-in. lengths of rigid copper pipe for the upper part of the dome
  - four $5/8$-in. x 17-in. lengths of curved soft copper tubing for the dome
- Copper fittings:
  - four $3/4$-in. Ts
  - four $3/4$-in. x $1/2$-in. x $3/4$-in. reducer Ts
  - four $1/2$-in. Ts
  - four $1/2$-in. 90° elbows

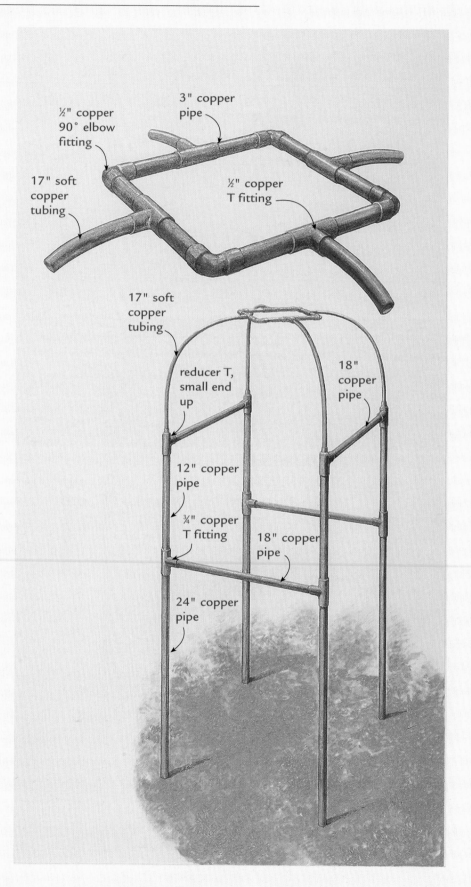

Copper is easy to work with, too. A few simple tools—including a pipe cutter and soldering torch—are all it takes. Using soft, easily bendable copper tubing to make curves, assorted lengths of pipe for straight sections, and T-shaped and 90-degree elbow fittings to join pipes together, building a garden structure is as easy as playing with Tinkertoys. My first trellis took just about three hours to build. The materials are inexpensive, too—my homemade trellis cost about $30, excluding tools.

To plan my trellis, I sketched a sample and used bamboo to build a model. Then I moved on to using copper, and with help from my brother, Terry, I built a trellis large enough—about 20 inches square and 4 feet high—to train a mature rosebush. That was just the start. Now I'm hooked on making copper garden structures. I have several different trellises, an arbor, and lots of ideas. The techniques I learned while building the trellis can be used to create just about anything. But it all started with this simple, basic structure.

CUT THE PIPE TO LENGTH

The first step is getting the materials ready, and that means using a pipe cutter to cut the copper pipes to size. Place the pipe between the tool's cutting wheel and its rollers, so that the cutting wheel hits the pipe where it should be cut. Turn the set screw to put pressure on the pipe. Keep the pressure gentle—too much can crush or crimp the pipe. Rotate the cutter around the pipe twice. This first cut scores the copper. Tighten the set screw a little more, and rotate the cutter twice around the pipe again. Repeat until the pipe has been cut through.

BEND AND CUT THE CURVES

For the curves, I use copper refrigerator coil instead of standard plumbing pipe. It's softer and bends more easily. It comes in a roll, and I simply uncoil some, measure along the curve, and cut off 17 inches. With soft tubing, it's even more important to make the cuts gently. Don't straighten out the tubing while measuring or cutting; it may crimp or dent. Once I've cut the piece to length, I bend it gently to a shape that is almost a quarter circle. Then I cut and bend three other pieces to match it.

CLEAN AND FLUX THE PIPES

After cutting the pipes, I use a nylon or metal cleaning pad to scour away any oxide from the ends of the pipe. Clean at least an inch at each end of the pipes.

Then, I don a pair of latex or rubber gloves and set up in a well-ventilated, bright work space to avoid fumes from the solder and flux. Brush a thin coat of soldering flux—a substance that helps create stronger bonds when soldering most metals—onto the end of any pipe that is to fit into a T-shaped, elbow-shaped, or other fitting. That means ½ inch of fluxing both ends of most pipes.

ASSEMBLE THE BASE

I start at the bottom of the trellis, fitting the top end of the four longest pipes into a T-shaped fitting. They should fit neatly. I connect shorter, upright pieces to the opposite side of the fitting, creating a pole about 38 inches long, with the T fitting near the middle and an 18-inch, horizontal bar to link two of the poles into H-shaped assemblies. I place reducer-T fittings at the top corners, and connect the two pieces with the second pair of 18-inch, horizontal crossbars. To help align all the pieces, I mark a 20-inch square

Cutting and Connecting Pipes

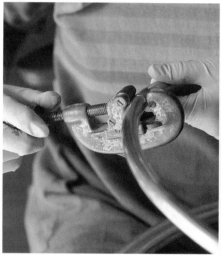

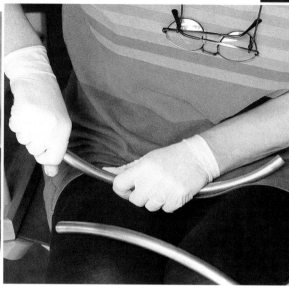

1 Don't hurry the pipe cutting. Tighten the set screw on the pipe cutter just a little at a time, or you risk crimping the pipe.

2 Gently bend the arched pieces to shape. It's easy to make an arch that's too tight, and difficult to correct it if you do.

3 Clean and flux the pipes, then put them together like Tinkertoys. T-shaped and elbow-shaped copper fittings make it easy to assemble the arbor.

on the garage floor, and use it as a guide for the base of the trellis.

ADD THE DOMED TOP

Because the square top is composed of so many short lengths of pipe joined with so many fittings, it's easier to work on this piece separately on a flat surface. To make the top, I flux the ends of each pipe and assemble four identical pieces, each with two 3-inch lengths of pipe joined by a T fitting in the middle. Then, using the elbow-shaped fittings, I join the four straight pieces into a square. The stem of each T fitting should face out in order to connect to the four curved pieces that link the square to the rest of the structure. The other end of the curved piece fits onto the small opening of the reducer T fittings on the base. I don't worry about making the dome perfect at this point.

SOLDER FROM THE BOTTOM UP

I usually turn the soldering over to my brother, Terry. He's an expert. I've done enough, though, to know soldering takes practice. I also know this project is very forgiving, and that it is easy to wipe off excess soft solder with a damp, cotton cloth.

Wearing his safety glasses, Terry works from the bottom of the trellis up, squaring or straightening each joint before applying solder. When the joint looks good, he uncoils an 8-inch length of solder; this keeps his hands away from hot pipes and the torch flame.

Then he lights the propane torch and starts heating the area he wants to solder. He moves the torch back and forth evenly across the fitting, never aiming it directly at a joint—it's too easy to burn off the flux. Flux is essential to a good bond, so if he does burn it away, he lets the joint cool, cleans the parts

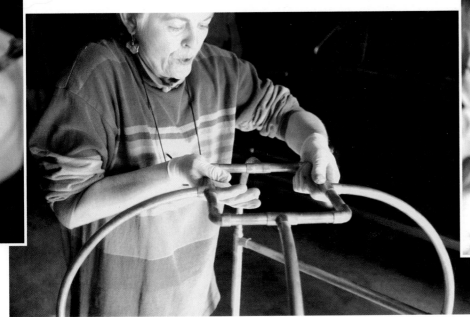

5 Use a torch to heat the fitting. When the copper is hot enough, touch the solder to that joint. The solder should melt and flow into place.

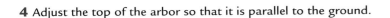

4 Adjust the top of the arbor so that it is parallel to the ground.

again with the scouring pad, reapplies the flux, and tries again.

When the flux starts to bubble, the temperature is just about right. He gives it a little more heat, then touches the solder to the joint; it melts on contact and flows smoothly into place. Any excess is wiped away. Pipes should always be handled with care—they can be very hot, even a foot or two from the fitting. The trick is to work slowly until you get the feel for it. It isn't necessary to make the joints watertight.

SQUARE OFF THE DOME

Once the upright and horizontal pieces have been soldered, adjust the curved pieces and the square top. Check by eye to make sure the curved pieces are arranged symmetrically and that the square top is parallel with the ground. After we adjust all the pieces, Terry

solders the dome joint by joint, checking to make sure that unsoldered pieces have not shifted. Once he's finished, I use a stiff wire brush to clean any excess solder and flux off the joints.

I like to let the copper age naturally. But if you cannot wait for the verdigris finish to appear, a faux verdigris paint will give it an aged look.

MOVE THE FINISHED TRELLIS TO THE GARDEN

Copper structures are easily installed in the garden. I take a 3-foot length of rebar and drive it 18 inches into the ground, then slip the copper pipe over the rebar. That's all there is to it. There's no need to pound in a piece of rebar for each of the four legs; two lengths of rebar fitted to two legs of the trellis should easily hold the structure in place.

FINISHING
TOUCHES

4

IN ADDITION TO THE LARGER architectural features within a garden, there are smaller ones that are also important, such as garden benches or edging treatments around a flower bed. Depending on how and where you use each of these, they can transcend their functional qualities and become design elements within a garden.

Many accents serve no function other than that they appeal to the gardener's sense of playfulness. When thinking about art objects in the garden, don't limit your thinking to expensive pieces of statuary. A group of rocks purposely arranged is a work of art that anyone can accomplish.

And while you're enjoying your garden, why not add the sound of water trickling down a manmade cascade or create a fountain from a garden container?

EVE THYRUM

gardens with her husband in Delaware, where she volunteers at the Scott Arboretum at Swarthmore College and is an active member of the Hardy Plant Society.

Ornaments
in the Garden

Site garden ornaments to complement surrounding garden spaces. In the author's garden, which is filled with more than 100 pieces of sculpture, two bronze herons find a home by a pond.

I LOVE TO EMBELLISH—my clothing, my house, and best of all, my garden. My first garden ornament, a beautiful copper owl, actually spent 12 years flying from coffee table to coffee table, as I repeatedly pronounced, "Someday, my friend, you will ornament my garden," a garden I had yet to create. When we did find land, and I began building the bones of the landscape, my special owl found its first outdoor home on a boulder near a terrace, only to move one year later to a newly created herb garden, and then to a pond edge, and finally, to a sunken knot garden. Somehow, my ornaments never do find permanent homes—my owl has been quite happy flying from one perch to another.

Our latest move has been into an area rich in gardening history. We bought a house situated in the middle of a 2¼-acre overgrown orchard with the idea that I would surrender my 18-year career in science to the challenge of growing green plants outdoors. Living near Longwood Gardens, I enrolled in its two-year program in ornamental horticulture, hoping to learn just what plants I could grow in this area and how to integrate them into the landscape. As a result, my love of gardening mushroomed into an obsession. And with it grew my desire to embellish what I had grown.

NATURE INSPIRES CREATIVITY

First we cleared our sloping landscape of its old fallen fruit trees, poison ivy, and multi flora roses. Rocks dominated the land, with many large outcroppings as well as mounds of smaller ones cast by farmers into the bordering hedgerow. The art of rock rearranging soon became an obsession with my husband, Per. Using winches and come-alongs, he moved boulders into artistic groupings, and rearranged them as terracing retainers and as low walls weaving through the landscape. He used rocks to depict stories, and even levitated some into the arms of a pollarded cherry.

Along with rock works, Per created five ponds: two terrace pools behind our house, a double pond nestled among large boulders on the hillside, a pool at the edge of a knot garden, and finally a large woodland pond anchored by a gazebo. And with water to play with, we brought statuary into the garden in the form of fountains. Frogs naturally populated our water gardens, and eventually they became a recurrent theme for ornament throughout the garden.

The garden has been developing and growing for more than 15 years. A series of island plantings and gardens, each individual unto themselves yet integrated into the overall design, forms the basis of the landscape. The garden is an informal one: no straight lines, no formal hedges, save the knot garden. It is

Motifs in the Garden

By developing motifs, the author creates a sense of unity in the garden. Wild, wonderful, and wacky birds add a whimsical and lighthearted tone. Further interest is created by partially hiding a bird from view so that it can be discovered (bottom left), by choosing rusty metal objects that blend naturally with the landscape (below), by positioning a striding ostrich in the middle of a large expanse of lawn so it can be seen from far away (top left), and by grouping similar objects together, like this family of storks dancing around a tree (right).

The author's husband, Per, takes great pleasure in creating ornament out of rocks. They are natural to the property and so artfully placed and arranged, they seem almost to come alive.

filled with both woody and herbaceous plants. I am a plant lover and a collector of all green things that are rare and unusual. I design with color, texture, form, and contrast in mind. As I developed each specific area of the garden, I introduced a touch of whimsy by adding unusual ornaments. I create the gardens to make people smile.

THEMES CREATE CONTINUITY

To incorporate my love of ornament into the garden, I soon realized that I needed themes to create a sense of continuity. I already had the rocks and water, a statuary collection centered around frogs and birds, sitting spaces carved into the landscape, and tropical plants summering outdoors in containers. By building on these specific themes, I relaxed and didn't worry about following traditional rules of ornament use in the garden. Whose rules are they, anyway? I was having a grand time, and that's what mattered most.

I find water is a pleasing and soothing element in the garden. Still water is calming—it reflects the sky as well as silhouettes of limbs overhead. Moving water is cooling, and a splashing fountain supplies music to its surroundings. We try to keep it simple—too much noise or movement is jarring to the eyes as well as to the ears. With water comes a host of living creatures—frogs, fish, birds, dragonflies, turtles, snakes, and water striders. Each pond lends itself to further embellishment: Bronze herons stand at the edge of a clump of pickerel weed (*Pontederia cordata*) and rusty metal birds perch near a stone wall, interplanted with Christmas ferns (*Polystichum acrostichoides*), hardy begonia (*Begonia grandis*), Japanese primroses (*Primula japonica*), and lots of moss (perfect sitting pads for the live frogs).

ORNAMENT ADDS
A LIGHTHEARTED NOTE

For me, an informal garden demands art that is fun rather than serious. The types of art I collect and create allow me to personalize the garden. I set a tone of lightheartedness, and when I enter the green space I feel instantly cheered and entertained. Even whimsical ornament, however, can serve purposeful design functions. It can be used as an anchor, giving a sense of solidity to an area, as a focal point to draw you into or through the garden, or as a complement to the texture and color of plants.

I rarely buy or create ornaments for a specific spot. One ornament came into the garden on my lap via an 18-hour plane ride from Japan because it spoke to me and just had to be part of my growing space. Others were plucked from dusty benches at the local flea market or fashioned from nature's abundance (an old, twining vine turned into a snake with the help of some copper eyes and fangs).

I have a few favorite artisans whose work I have collected over the years. Bill Heise, from Vermont, is a creator of found-metal sculpture. I have a marvelous collection of his birds—bitterns, secretaries, herons, and sandpipers. An artist from Pennsylvania who is simply named Simple uses a laser torch to cut out two-dimensional iron objects ranging in size from 2 to 5 feet. I have collected a series of his birds, painted in bold colors. I use them as focal points in the landscape, and I love to plant colorful gardens around them. Three bright-blue herons with magenta heads and yellow bills are surrounded by rosy-purple smoke bush (*Cotinus coggygria*

'Velvet Cloak'), brilliant yellow golden creeping Jenny (*Lysimachia nummularia* 'Aurea'), and the bright-pink blooms of hydrangea (*Hydrangea macrophylla* 'Pia').

I also think of furniture as ornament in the garden because it can be as beautiful to look at as it is functional. I use it not only on the terraces or in groupings beside the large pond, but also by associating it with secret hideaways or open vistas. By carefully limbing up trees and tucking in chairs and tables, I have spots to wind down my gardening day with a well-earned bottle of cold beer. Shafts of late-day sunlight squeeze through the trees as I watch a busy wren building her nest. Or I place a bench at the start of a long vista, and many a morning I sip coffee there, smelling

Many fountains adorn the garden's ponds, and frogs are a favorite theme. A beautiful bench is nestled along the far side of the pond—the perfect place to enjoy morning coffee.

> *"I soon realized that I needed themes to create a sense of continuity."*

the garden and savoring the view. Weathered teak and cedar are the furniture materials of choice, blending nicely into the landscape.

DISPLAY POTS IN ODD-NUMBERED GROUPINGS

I display a collection of urns; some are empty and others are filled with tender perennials and tropicals. The containers are either unglazed terra-cotta from Italy and Mexico or a single-color glazed clay from Southeast Asia. I use about 130 containers, and try to make them harmonize with one another in shape, size, and color. The ones filled with plantings are placed on two terraces, where they complement the hard lines of bricks. The containers add a splash of color on a sunny terrace and a lushness of cool green to a shady terrace. I use them in groups of three, five, or more, adding height to the display with pedestals.

A selection of old Turkish jars filled with *Echeveria*, *Agave*, and *Gasteria* species adorn the edge of the rectangular pond by the knot garden. They clearly help soften the look of the hardscaping. Elsewhere, unplanted urns—large Turkish oil jars or terra-cotta African vessels—find spots next to plantings of irises or grasses and in a border of mixed shrubs.

KEEP IT ALL IN GOOD TASTE

How do you incorporate 140 pieces of sculpture; 15 groupings of furniture; 42 birdhouses, feeders, and birdbaths; 15 urns; and 130 potted containers into a 2-acre landscape? There is a fine line between tasteful and tacky, and I try constantly not to overstep this boundary.

Part of the secret is to keep things simple. I usually place art singly, as an enhancement or complement to the surrounding garden space, though I will place ornaments in groups if they are of similar design, color, or material. I like to soften the edges of ornaments with plants to make them an integral part of the garden. Much of the artwork is made of rusty metal, a form that blends naturally into the landscape.

I also think about the element of spacing. I strive to site ornaments in interesting ways so visitors are either urged to move from one area of the garden to the next or given cause to pause. Surprises are fun, so I site statuary where it can be discovered, or I shield it from constant view, among foliage, around a corner, behind the viewer, or above. I place small frogs under hosta leaves, a striding ostrich on unmown lawn in the middle of a large expanse, a rusty opossum along a branch of a Chinese chestnut, and a leaping gazelle camouflaged behind spiky boulders.

I find the best use of ornament is sometimes unplanned—the blue flowers of *Clematis* × *durandii* peeking out from under the wing of a blue and yellow whimsical canary, or *Asarina scandens*, with its dainty snapdragonlike blooms, twining up and around the long leg of a rusting metal heron. I never assume that an ornament has been placed in a permanent and perfect spot. One of the great pleasures of a garden is that it grows, evolves, and changes. Moving ornaments to different locations keeps the garden dynamic and refreshing. Ask my owl.

Site ornaments where they can be discovered. This eclectic grouping of birds and birdhouses is partially hidden behind a planting of tall conifers.

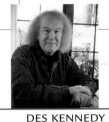

DES KENNEDY

gardens on Denman
Island, British Columbia,
Canada. He writes and
lectures about gardening
across Canada and in the
United States.

Pool *and* Cascade

A cascade of small waterfalls and pools tumbles artfully over sandstone rocks and concrete, lending sound and motion to the author's hillside garden. The pink foxgloves at right tower over low rock garden plants.

THE SWEET DELIGHTS of running water in a garden have always attracted me. Whether minuscule or massive, a watercourse offers unique pleasures—the enchanting trickle of water over stone, the meditative calm of plants and sky glimpsed in a reflecting pool, the charm of songbirds splashing at water's edge.

Yet of all the garden projects I've longed to try, none seemed so intimidating as the watercourse that my companion, Sandy, and I eventually built with ease. We were daunted not by the scale of the cascade (a series of small waterfalls), nor by the amount of grunt labor involved, but by the challenge of capturing that elusive element, water, to make it give up its wild wanderings and behave according to human plans. And we were confused by conflicting information about design and construction from various "experts."

Seen up close, small waterfalls seem to spring from the rocks. A green-and-white hosta in the foreground provides a bright focal point amid the many shades of green and the small flowers of the rock garden.

We learned in the making that a watercourse requires forethought in design and care in execution, but almost anyone can do it. Although our project might appear at first glance a tad grand for some backyard do-it-yourselfers, the spill of water and the pool are actually quite small. In any case, since the principles of making water features like these remain the same no matter what size project you're planning, you could easily adapt what we did to an even smaller scale.

Before you plan a water feature, do some research. We consulted books and magazine articles and encountered a bewildering diversity of opinion. Read whatever you can lay your hands on—but read each article as just one more opinion. Check your local building codes. Finally, seek out the advice of people in your area who've had experience constructing a pool or cascade. Sandy's father had constructed a lovely miniature cascade a few years back. He provided helpful hints as well as an example to follow and thereby prove myself a fellow worthy of his daughter.

SITE IT NEAR YOUR HOUSE

There are several things to consider before you site a water feature. Try to keep it near the house so you can enjoy the sight and sound of water at all hours. There you'll have ready access to electricity for the pump and to water for filling the pool. If you plan to grow aquatic plants, which require full sun for blooming, avoid heavily shaded sites. Steer clear of overhanging deciduous trees—cleaning their fallen leaves out of the water every autumn is a nuisance.

For us, siting was a simple matter since we had a small hillside—about 8 feet in vertical

"A watercourse requires forethought in design and care in execution, but almost anyone can do it."

drop—close to the house. We decided to develop a rock garden on the hillside and have a small cascade thread its way through the rocks, with short waterfalls spilling into small pools and finally into a larger pool at the bottom.

If you're not blessed with a hillside but still want a cascade, you can create an artificial grade. Even a small spill can be very effective, and you can create it with no wasted effort by mounding up the earth excavated from the pool. For a larger hill, start with rock or rubble and cover it with earth.

DESIGN INSPIRED BY NATURE

Nature is a marvelous instructress. A few hours spent contemplating the spill of water along a brook near our home revealed the secrets of how water cascades over stone, hollows out small pools, undercuts banks, and glistens over gravel. Soothed by the beauty of water and excited by its possibilities, we decided to have our cascade meander and trickle down the hill rather than drop dramatically and noisily, and to make it look as if it had occurred naturally, rather than by human contrivance.

It's important that the scale of the cascade—the volume of water and the size of the pools along it—is appropriate for the size of the hill, the rocks you use, and nearby plantings. A tiny trickle can disappear among huge boulders, large shrubs, and trees. Similarly, an aggressive torrent will overwhelm alpines

The author checks a groove that he just chiseled in the rock to the left of his hand. The sharp lip of the rock sends water falling cleanly onto the spillway just below.

or other miniature plantings. I don't believe there's a rule of thumb for figuring proper scale—you must rely on intuition, common sense, and the lessons of nature. Because our cascade runs through a rock garden planted with small plants, we opted for a low-volume water flow.

Scale also affects cost. A cascade like ours needs a pump to lift water from the bottom to the top of the watercourse. The higher the lift and the more water running in a cascade, the larger and more expensive the pump.

Apart from the question of apt proportion, there are some other considerations. Several small waterfalls of different heights create an interesting diversity in the "soundscape," more than one or two loud splashers would. Above all, if young children frequent the area, you should fence it off or keep a close eye on them.

We made the bottom pool about 6 feet in diameter—just large enough for water gardening if we decide to take it up. If you plan to include fish or aquatic plants in your pool, make it 18 to 24 inches deep. Deeper pools can be designed with edge shelves or islands about 18 inches below water level on which tubs of water lilies can be placed. Most aquatic plants prefer relatively calm, warm water. You can't expect them to thrive in a pool that is frothing from a torrent. To accommodate both a cascade and aquatic plants, you'll need separate pools or a single pool large enough to absorb a cascade at one end while remaining calm at the other.

TEST YOUR WATERFALL AS YOU GO

We began construction by moving earth around the hillside to about the contours we wanted. Next I buried a section of 1½-inch-diameter black polyethylene water pipe, running it from the bottom pool to the top of the hill. Through it, I would insert—and remove for repairs, if necessary—a ½-inch diameter polyethylene pipe to carry water from the bottom pool to the top pool.

I started building the cascade from the bottom and steepest part of the hill, making three small waterfalls and pools almost directly above one another. Higher up, the grade lessened, and I included a short, 4-inch deep spillway between each waterfall and pool.

I constructed each waterfall with a flat, overhanging rock and then poured a bucketful of water along the watercourse to see how it would spill from the overhang. With certain stubborn rocks, I had to hand-chisel a pathway for the water; on others I had to undercut the lip of the overhang to prevent the water from running back along its underside.

I lined the pools and the spillways between them with three layers of material—first newspaper, then heavy plastic and, finally, a topping of concrete 2 inches thick. The newspaper protects the plastic from punctures, and the plastic prevents leaks. I extended the plastic several inches onto the overhanging rock at each waterfall and applied a

sealer to the set concrete. With more bucketsful of water, I tested the splash of each waterfall to ensure that the receiving pool was wide enough.

I outlined the shape of the bottom pool with a piece of thick rope and set to digging. Unfortunately, in my zeal to have the pool appear natural, I included so many squiggles and wiggles that the excavation looked more like a piece of a jigsaw puzzle than anything from nature. A few more hours of work produced a gently curved hole about 2 feet deep in the center with gradually sloping sides.

WATERPROOF THE POOL

Despite the false start, digging the hole was a simple matter compared with the agony of trying to decide how to waterproof the pool. The fundamental choices are concrete, prefabricated fiberglass, and plastic sheeting (also called pool liner). Concrete pools require considerable skill and labor, and if improperly constructed, especially in a climate where the ground freezes, are prone to cracking. Fiberglass shells are durable and idiot-proof, but they're also rather pricey and look unavoidably artificial. (Prefabricated fiberglass cascade pieces are also available, with the same pluses and minuses.) Plastic sheeting is relatively inexpensive and easy to install, impervious to freezing and not glaringly artificial looking. But pool liners are also easy to puncture and have a limited lifespan—between 10 and 40 years, depending upon their thickness.

I chose a pool liner. A simple formula determines the required length and width of the liner. Add twice the depth plus twice the edge detail (a minimum 6 inches overlap at pool edge) to the length and to the width of the excavation. My 20-mil pond liner is

10 feet square. Some pond supply companies will make a liner to your specifications. It's more expensive, but it fits more snugly.

Before laying the liner, we precisely leveled the pool edges to prevent creating an unsightly patch of exposed pool liner on the high side. We also removed sharp stones from the excavation and lined it with a 1-inch thickness of newspaper to protect the liner against puncturing. (A thick layer of sand works, too.) Then we unfolded the liner in the pool, allowing it to relax into the contours. After anchoring the perimeter of the liner with heavy rocks, we filled the pool with water to compress the liner into all the corners of the excavation, gently spreading and smoothing out bulges in the liner by hand. I trimmed the corners and stored the excess for possible future patches. Then I laid large sandstone slabs around the pool perimeter so they covered the liner edge, using rocks that could overhang the edge without tumbling in.

SELECT THE RIGHT PUMP

Choosing the right pump for our cascade was easy. Pump dealers or water garden suppliers carry an assortment of small, submersible pumps specially designed for water gardens. They're rated by gallons-per-minute and vertical lifts. To figure the flow I needed, I put a garden hose at the top of our cascade and played with different volumes of water until I found a pleasing rate. Then I stuck the hose into a five-gallon bucket, timed how long it took to fill the bucket, and divided the time by five to get the gallons-per-minute rate.

I tucked our pump beneath an overhanging rock on a raised shelf of soil that I made when I was excavating. (The pump works best if it's not at the pool bottom, where debris collects.) Also, the pump is easily accessible for repairs and removal.

Mixing electricity and water can be a high-risk business, and you should take particular care to follow the safety guidelines that come with your pump. A pool is no place for some haywire extension-cord arrangement. We hired an electrician to run a power line through a protective piece of underground pipe from the house electrical panel to a poolside receptacle for which I fashioned a small, concrete, waterproof housing. We protected the line with a ground-fault interrupter circuit (GFIC), which automatically cuts off electricity when there's a voltage leak. You can buy a GFIC (which is required by the U.S. National Electric Code) from your local electrical-supplies dealer.

After what seemed like months of planning, heaving around rocks and earth, hard decision-making, and experimentation, the day at last dawned when our cascade and pool were completed. We plugged in the pump. We waited, trembling with anticipation, and yes, there it came: a tentative trickle, then stronger, growing to a boisterous splashing and gurgling, a playful, exuberant, lovely little cascade, tinkling and whispering through the garden. What fun! We pictured ourselves reclining lazily by poolside during the dog days of summer, soothed, refreshed, and rewarded by the sweet, cool splash of water.

This view from the top of the cascade shows a spillway and several small pools lined with plastic and newspaper. The author is pouring sandstone-colored concrete on the plastic of the lowest small pool.

VIRGINIA SMALL

is a *Fine Gardening* associate editor and nationally published poet. She accentuates the sculptural effects of many rock outcrops in her garden in northwestern Connecticut.

Accentuate Art *in the* Garden

Foliage forms a fitting frame for this bust of Salvador Dali by Dennis Fairweather. The statue graces his garden in Norfolk, England.

FOR SEVERAL YEARS, a painted female figure in the shape of a straight-backed chair graced my patio garden. Her lifelike presence amid the ficus and fuchsia startled, amused, and provoked interaction. Rarely was she ignored. Last year, when I moved from Florida to Connecticut, I gave my garden sentinel to a friend who had been especially fond of this sculpture and was delighted to place it in her garden.

As a lifelong art lover, I am ever drawn to interesting art, especially in garden settings. There's something intriguing about seeing creative objects nestled or looming in open-air showcases, surrounded by plants, and exposed to the elements.

ART ENRICHES BOTH GARDENS AND GARDENERS

While gardens are often works of art in themselves, art objects can increase the subtlety, splendor, and enjoy-

Lubomir Tomaszewski draws inspiration from decayed trees to create sculptures. This wood-and-metal "Orpheus" melds into the artist's wooded garden located in Easton, Connecticut.

ment of a garden. Well-placed focal points draw visitors along pathways or serve as graceful spurs to contemplation. Fountains, mobiles, wind chimes, and light reflectors or refractors expand the sensory experience of a garden. Structural elements, such as gates, pillars, friezes, and tilework, can unify a garden and give it an inimitable sense of style. Art objects might take viewers by surprise, even take their breath away. And the makers of gardens with art invariably seem enchanted by the interplay between their special objects and nature.

Jim York's entire garden in Newtown, Connecticut, is an all-season, outdoor gallery for a whimsical and eclectic collection of art. Meandering the curved pathways of this hillside garden, I feel like Dorothy in Oz. Fanciful art objects of varying sizes and motifs can be glimpsed from nearly any point. A massive abstract mobile by Nick Barzetti twirls overhead; a 15-foot, painted-metal giraffe by Emil Racenet towers above a bed of daylilies; a stained-glass mosaic of a human figure lies embedded in the soil. Suddenly, I chance upon a Tin Man holding court beneath a willow. This lushly planted—and embellished—garden exudes a spirit of unbridled playfulness. And Jim York, a former gallery owner, admits he relishes moving each object until it seems "in the right place."

Pamela and Don Michaelis of Albuquerque, New Mexico, both publishers, began collecting artwork for their garden after gracing their entire home with original art. Their sculptures range from a life-sized, stylized ceramic fertility goddess by Beverly Magennis in the center of a sun-shielding pergola, to a pair of silhouetted, chrome-plated chickens by Bob Haozous that reflect colorful bedding plants. Pamela says they spend more time outside now, enthralled with how some pieces catch light or cast shadows or simply enjoying the mood a piece inspires. They also cherish the intriguing views from inside when the garden is dormant.

Sculptor and teacher Leslie Fry of Winooski, Vermont, found that her life and her art changed dramatically five years ago when she bought a home with an expansive yard. "I turned into a maniac gardener overnight, and suddenly I started making art for my garden instead of for gallery spaces." Now she creates open-framed metal sculptures for vines to climb over and into, as well as small, cast-concrete structures that become part of "miniature landscapes." She encourages moss and lichen to grow on some pieces so that they become "living objects that interact with the landscape." Discoveries gleaned while gardening now shape her experiments with new artistic media.

A fountain sculpture by Keeyla Meadows serves as a focal point in the artist's garden. She uses vibrant plants to play off the hues in the copper-and-ceramic frieze.

Whimsy wears well in outdoor settings. Jim York created a garden room to spotlight his collection of belt-embellished elm trunks.

CREATIVE STRATEGIES
FOR PLACING ART

What makes art "work" in a garden setting? How do gardeners fashion a harmonious outdoor home for special objects? Albuquerque artist and former landscape designer Robert Hooton says gardens are "all about three-dimensional space. You can't just drop objects into that space. You have to consider the scale and forms of all the surrounding elements. I like to create vistas by combining art with plants that will make an attractive base or background." His garden has what he calls a "minimalist Zen approach," with places for rest, contemplation, and interaction.

For artist and garden designer Keeyla Meadows of Albany, California, color is the strongest element she works with in bringing art into a garden. The painter and ceramist prefers placing vibrant sculpture or ceramic pieces in naturalistic gardens. "I use art to bring focus to certain areas and to play off the colors, shapes, and textures of the surrounding plants, as well as the furniture. I like these various elements to resonate and bounce off each other." After she discovers or makes a piece of art, she usually finds herself "going on a treasure hunt for plants with similar or compatible hues to go with it."

In contrast, gallery owner John Cram of Asheville, North Carolina, says he's "a big fan of putting art in the landscape that can recede or come back into view." One such piece, a long, rusted-iron "fence" of running figures by Judie Bomberger, often blends into the hedge behind it, depending on the light. While his contemporary home features

Nestled among layers of foliage, a giant leaf teases the eyes of viewers. Artists George Little and David Lewis of Bainbridge Island, Washington, sculpt naturalistic objects from concrete.

Cherubic figures balance a burst of blooms. Kate Emery of Farmington, Connecticut, uses statuary as the focal point of a garden with a formal framework.

Lush plantings shelter a carved-stone sculpture by Marcia Donahue. Bob Clark and Raul Zumba weave eclectic art throughout their Oakland, California, garden.

When Paul Hennen places a large-scale classical sculpture in his Pomfret, Connecticut, garden, he thinks about how it will be viewed from many vantages, including during winter. "While something might be the focal point in one area, I like it to be partially visible from other places, enticing you to go around a corner to see it." The retired army officer carefully sited a half dozen large figures in several garden rooms. He customizes molds to cast concrete pieces to his own liking.

COLLECT WHAT YOU LOVE, THEN MAKE A HOME FOR IT

The guideline I keep hearing from gardeners enamored with art is that they only collect pieces that move them. Elizabeth Gibson Wakeman, an interior designer and avid gardener in Sarasota, Florida, advises finding "something that you absolutely love that won't fit inside. Then decide what colors and shapes will enhance it, and start planting." Pamela Michaelis agrees. "Whenever we discover a piece that excites us that can go outside, we buy it, and worry later about where to put it."

boldly colorful art, his gardens showcase mostly monochromatic metal or wood sculptures. He also tends to place art near the house where it's most visible. He designed one of his favorite niches, a water garden with a fountain and two sculptures, to be viewed from a wall-sized window as well as from outside. Perhaps his most dramatic—yet subtle—sculpture has roots deep in the earth. He wanted to create more light in his mostly shaded garden. Rather than cut down an old oak tree, he commissioned chainsaw artist Roger Cochran to use the tree as raw material. Now, a family of black bears scurries up the 18-foot trunk.

Original art, especially by local artists, can be quite affordable. Often you can find one-of-a-kind artwork for less than mass-produced statuary. Some collectors place certain art objects in the garden knowing they will eventually disintegrate, just as plants run their course. To counter the elements, the Michaelises coat metal sculptures with a spray lubricant a few times a year to enhance the patina and to clean away dirt. John Cram uses boiled linseed oil thinned with turpentine to coat wood or metal sculptures and to deepen the hue.

"Well-placed focal points draw visitors along pathways or serve as graceful spurs to contemplation."

FINDING A PERFECT PLACE FOR FOUND ART

Many collectors of garden art eventually dabble with placing found objects in their gardens. One of Don Michaelis' favorite "sculptures" is a small, rusted coil spring he found and strategically placed in a low bed of cacti and succulents. Other gardeners artfully arrange stones, shells, and other natural objects.

Sometimes "found art" takes on a life of its own. Several years ago, Jim York playfully turned the trunk of an elm tree into a torso by inverting it and placing a belt around it. One creation led to another, and now he has a whole collection, all with expressive belts.

He recently ripped out a corner of lawn and created a separate garden room for the gang of about 30 figures. He says most people can't help laughing when they see them, and Jim is continually amused by what he calls his "audience."

Whether abstract or realistic, fanciful or contemplative, art objects stretch the parameters of a garden. My new favorite piece of garden art hangs near the house in a pine tree in a secluded seating area. The V-shaped mobile, made from copper and electrical metallic tubing, catches glints of sunlight and sings when the wind kicks up. I often enjoy its music even when I'm not in the garden.

Larger-than-life sunbathers rest amid a billowy blanket of chartreuse lady's mantle. This Katy McFadden piece is displayed in Barbara Blossom Ashmun's garden in Portland, Oregon.

AURELIA SCOTT,
a Master Gardener, can be found weeding the lavender in her Portland, Maine, garden, where she is also an avid bird-watcher.

Sundials
Lend a Sense of
Time

(OPPOSITE) This horizontal sundial is unusual in that its gnomon is in the shape of a loop.
(INSET) This sundial placed on a pedestal anchors an herbal knot garden.

W HEN I WAS a child, my father positioned a sundial on a pedestal in the side yard. He set it near a young weeping willow tree, which, as it grew, shielded the sundial from the light it needed to reveal the time. Despite this, I spent many hours under the arc of those willow branches imagining a once-upon-a-time world in which passing hours were recorded in triangles of shade.

SUNDIALS DATE FROM 1500 B.C.

Once-upon-a-time indeed, for sundials are an ancient method of telling time. The oldest known was constructed in Egypt around 1500 B.C. It was shaped like an L, and the length of the shadow cast by the vertical leg along the horizontal leg indicated the time. Romans perfected the horizontal sundial we know today, and even invented portable versions for traveling. By the 1st century B.C.,

143

A sundial mounted on a pedestal is eye-catching, so make sure you position one near an interesting feature or amidst some colorful flower clusters.

Equatorial sundials work just as well in the garden as horizontal ones. The rod in the center serves as the gnomon.

so many sundials were erected in Rome that one citizen wrote, "Let the gods damn the first man... who set up a sundial in this city... He has chopped the day into slices."

During the Renaissance, sundials of every description were produced. In addition to marking hours and minutes, some sundials recorded the date, seasons, and signs of the Zodiac. Some even carried tide tables, which indicated the time of high tide at named ports when the moon was observed in a certain position. Those who couldn't afford their own sundials had only to look up as they walked, for vertical sundials were mounted on the outside walls of many churches and public buildings.

By the 16th century, though, increasingly efficient clocks began to supersede shadow-chasing sundials. Still, the French railway regulated its clocks by sundials until the end of the 19th century.

Gardeners, of course, don't need to mourn the passing of shadow clocks. We can perpetuate the 3,500-year tradition simply by placing a sundial in a sunny spot in the yard. Set on a stone pedestal, a sundial can both anchor the garden and trace the hours we spend digging.

Not only did the Romans perfect sundials as we know them today, but they were also among the first to use them in gardens. Roman gardens were private spaces, most often set behind houses and enclosed on all sides by colonnades and rooms. Plants were grown in 2- to 3-foot-high raised beds. In the midst of this ordered scene was the sundial—set in the courtyard on a raised, stone pedestal to catch the shadow of the sun god Sol as he crossed the sky.

After the Romans conquered ancient Britain, they took their sundials, as well as lettuce, roses, lilies, and violets, with them. When the Roman Empire collapsed in the 5th century, monasteries preserved Roman horticultural practices as well as their sundials. So today, when we set our sundial at the center of an herb parterre or along an allée of scented roses, we are following a practice that is centuries old.

Choose a sunny, spot when positioning your sundial.

HORIZONTAL AND EQUATORIAL SUNDIALS BEST FOR GARDENS

Of the eight categories of sundials, horizontal and equatorial are best suited for garden use. Horizontal sundials, the type commonly seen on pedestals, consist of a dial plate, marked in hour lines, and a "gnomon," the raised projection that casts a shadow. Equatorial sundials, which look like large, open globes, have the dial plate fixed in the plane of the equator; the gnomon takes the form of a rod set perpendicular to the dial.

Other sundials don't work as well in the garden for various reasons. Vertical sundials need to be attached to a wall, and other types of fixed sundials (polar, analemmatic, reflected ceiling) are difficult to find commercially and can be hard to read. Portable sundials work well, but as their name implies, they need to be carried about.

The sundial in the Smithsonian Institution's Enid A. Haupt Garden is one example of a lovely, handmade horizontal sundial. Mass-produced sundials are also widely available.

SUNDIALS WORK ACCORDING TO THE EARTH'S ROTATION

The principle behind sundials is simple. As the Earth rotates on its axis, the sun appears to move across the sky. Thus, the shadow of a gnomon placed parallel to the Earth's axis and pointing toward the celestial pole will move around itself in accordance to the sun's movement. The sun travels 15 degrees westward every hour; the gnomon's shadow on the sundial plate moves at the same rate. You read the time on a sundial by noting the hour line closest to the edge of the shadow. To be accurate, a sundial should be designed for the location where it will be used.

When choosing a site for a functional sundial, select a sunny, level spot. A sundial set atop a pedestal draws the eye upward, so ideally you should position one in the line of sight of an interesting feature—a path between flower beds, perhaps, or in front of a trellis, a flowering tree, or, simply, a wonderful view. Alternatively, use the sundial as a focal point, with triangular garden beds and paths radiating out from it. And make sure you set a bench nearby, so you can rest while contemplating Sol's journey from dawn's awakening to dusk's sleep.

Use a sundial as a focal point, with interesting beds and maze-like pathways radiating outward from it.

A Fountain
of Soothing
Sounds

STEVE SILK

is a *Fine Gardening* contributing editor whose passion for gardening includes photography, lecturing, and crafting outdoor furniture and ornaments for use in the garden.

Water spills out of a ceramic container, delighting the author with the sound of water in his garden.

I'VE ALWAYS LOVED the sound of a rushing stream. Whether I'm dry-fly fishing a gentle riffle or paddling a kayak through a roaring rapid, the music of moving water always has, for me, a restorative power. So when I started spending most of my time up to the elbows in garden soil, I discovered a simple way to bring that sound into the garden—one that requires little more than an afternoon's work, a handsome container, a piece of pond liner, a fair-sized plastic bucket, a pump, and a few other odds and ends.

The plan was simple: Water would spill from the mouth of a ceramic container and tumble over the stones into an underground reservoir, where a purring pump would boost the water back to the urn to continue the cycle. Getting the look and the sound right took a bit of tinkering, but now, whether I'm making my morning garden rounds, swaying in the hammock, or listening to the

147

hoots of barred owls at night, my fountain keeps me company, and my favorite music plays on.

PUT YOUR FOUNTAIN NEAR A FAVORITE SPOT

Once I decided to bring the sound of moving water into my garden, I soon realized that the best place to put it would be near one of my favorite seating spots. Then, whenever I sat down, I would be within earshot of my wasserspiele, and the sense of relaxation would be that much more complete.

There's another crucial factor to consider: electricity. You can locate the fountain near an existing outdoor outlet, or have an electrician run an underground wire out to your site and install an outlet. Electricity and water can be a dangerous combination, so be sure to use ground-fault interrupter circuitry. Avoid using extension cords; they'll just be something to trip over.

I like garden structures that look as if they belong in the garden, and thought a fountain with a classical look would complement my garden's formal framework. But since my plantings are anything but formal, I wanted something that wasn't too prim, something with an archaeological feel, like a Greek ruin. I wasn't planning to re-create the Parthenon, but I thought a neat-looking urn shaped like an amphora—a clay wine vessel—would do nicely. I'd lay the urn on its side atop some stones, as if it had simply fallen into place.

Piecing Together a Fountain of Sound

MATERIALS

- ⁕ Ceramic urn, vase, or other container *for use as the fountain.*
- ⁕ Plastic container *for use as an underground reservoir. One the size of a half-whiskey barrel is best.*
- ⁕ Electrical outlet *fitted with a ground-fault interrupter circuit.*
- ⁕ Pond liner: *a 6-foot by 6-foot piece should be plenty.*
- ⁕ Support: *metal grill or mesh and lengths of wood or iron to use for reinforcement.*
- ⁕ Recirculating pump *with a capacity of at least 300 gallons per hour.*
- ⁕ Plastic tubing *sized to connect to the pump. To see how much to buy, measure from the bottom of the reservoir to the top of the container and add about 3 feet.*
- ⁕ PVC pipe *large enough for the pump's cord and plug.*
- ⁕ Plumber's putty or silicon caulk
- ⁕ Hose clamp *to fit the plastic tubing. This can be used to reduce the flow of water, if desired.*
- ⁕ Ornamental stones
- ⁕ Shredded bark mulch

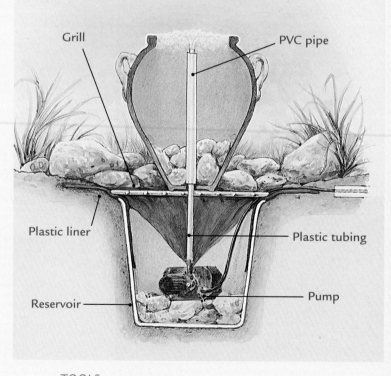

TOOLS

- ⁕ Razor knife, saw, screwdriver, and shovel

If my garden were cottagey, I might opt for a brightly colored container. Bamboo could be used to make a Japanese-style fountain. For an elemental look, let the water burst, geyser-like, from a bed of stones.

MOST OF THE PARTS GO UNDERGROUND

I like to think of this fountain as an illusion: a seemingly endless stream of water gushes from the container and disappears underground. The functional hardware that makes it all work is hidden in an underground reservoir that holds and recycles water and that contains the recirculating pump. I successfully used a 5-gallon bucket as a reservoir, but the larger volume of a plastic container intended for use as a liner for a half whiskey barrel would make a more efficient system.

Dig a hole large enough to accommodate the reservoir and deep enough so that the uppermost lip of the container will be a few inches below grade. Make sure the container is perfectly level in its underground home, then gently scrape away the earth above the lip to create a sort of soil funnel. Lay down a piece of pond liner big enough to cover the reservoir and the outermost margins of the soil funnel. Then, directly over the reservoir, cut an "X" a little smaller than the diameter of the reservoir. Let the flaps fall into the reservoir. The aim is to direct water splashing out of the fountain back to the reservoir. Ideally, the system shouldn't lose any water at all, other than through evaporation, even if the pump is on for days.

With the reservoir and the pond liner in place, clean any debris out of the reservoir, throw in a few small rocks, and drop in the pump. Any recirculating pump designed for water gardens will work, but one with a capacity of less than 300 gallons an hour won't

Thread the water line through the grill that supports the fountain, and then through a hole in the bottom of the container. Boards can be used to help stabilize the grill.

make much of a sound. I run the pump's electrical cord out through PVC pipe, which can be buried under a few inches of soil. That way I won't accidentally sever the wire, or worse, get electrocuted, while digging.

With the wire out of the way, connect a suitably-sized plastic tube to the pump's outlet, making sure it will be long enough to run up out of the reservoir and into the container. A tube that's a few extra feet long will give you more options later, when you're fine tuning the fountain's flow.

Now comes the only part of construction that's at all tricky—placing a strong but

Tubing runs up from the pump through the reservoir cover and into the container through the drainage hole.

Test the fountain's flow before covering the grill with stones.

porous cover over the reservoir. It must be sturdy enough to support your container, even when it's full of water. The metal grate of a charcoal grill works fine. You could also use a sturdy metallic mesh braced by lengths of wood or steel. It doesn't matter what the support looks like, since it will be hidden when you're finished. Make sure it's firmly in place before proceeding—you don't want the fountain toppling over. Run the tube up from the pump and through the porous support before you finish getting it in place.

A LITTLE TINKERING GETS THE SOUND RIGHT

Once the support system is secure, run the free end of the tube through the drainage hole in the container, then set the container in place. If your perfect piece of pottery doesn't have a drainage hole in the bottom, drill one—very carefully—with a masonry bit a little larger than the diameter of the plastic tube. When the tube has been threaded, seal the drainage hole tightly with plumber's putty or silicon caulk. If you use the silicon, allow several days for it to dry.

Position the container, turn on the pump, and see what happens. Unless you're incredibly lucky, the apparatus will need fine tuning to get the effect you want. Try tilting the container this way or that, fiddling with the

tube's position, pinching the tube to alter the flow of water, or moving the tube's end nearer to and farther from the container's mouth. Nearer the mouth, the stream of water is more like a geyser; farther away, the stream seems to just bubble up. Once you find the right spot, cut the tube to the desired length and keep it in position by filling the space between it and the wall of the container with small stones, or by using PVC piping as a sleeve over the tubing.

The testing stage was when I saw my original idea needed a total overhaul. No matter what I did, water wouldn't pour smoothly out of the sidelong urn—it just dribbled. I wound up standing the urn on end and letting the water gush out the top. This new arrangement didn't match my original vision, but it looked good and, more importantly, it sounded great.

FILL THE FOUNTAIN EACH TIME YOU USE IT

Once I'd given the fountain a pleasing look and sound, there was little left to do but cover my tracks. I used a jumble of river-worn stones to cover the support system and shredded bark mulch to further disguise the boundaries between garden and fountain. To finish the scene, I added some plants—*Heuchera* 'Pewter Veil', a few woodland ferns, and some liriope—selected for a long season of good looks.

My fountain doesn't require much maintenance, but every time I turn the pump on, I first fill the system to overflowing. And, if I leave the fountain running for a couple days, I periodically check to make sure there's plenty of water in the system. If it runs dry, the pump is doomed. In winter, I empty all the water and bring the pump and container inside so they won't be harmed by alternate freezes and thaws. Doing that ensures my little fountain will play on and on and on.

AURELIA SCOTT,
Master Gardener, can be
found weeding the laven-
der in her Portland,
Maine, garden, where
she is also an avid
birdwatcher.

Birdhouses
Attract Wildlife

U NION, MAINE, is reputed to have the
largest bluebird population in the state.
Why do these azure-winged birds flock
to a small town in the middle of Maine?
The answer is simple: It has what birds
want—clean air, clean water, and plenty of berries and garden bugs to eat. And, oh yes, a birdhouse on every corner.
You see, in Union, street signs double as birdhouses. A
long street name means a big birdhouse, a short street
name means a small birdhouse, a mid-sized street
name...you get the point.

CAVITY-NESTING BIRDS NEED HELP

We have cause to be concerned about the welfare of
native birds. Birds, like the bluebird, that nest in the cavities of dead and decaying trees are often left homeless as

The size of the nest box entrance will
determine which birds can use the house.

Putting up a birdhouse is an easy way to replace lost nesting places, as well as to increase the variety of birds that will visit your garden.

> *"Providing homes for birds ensures that I have year-round allies in my battle with garden pests."*

forests and open spaces are transformed into suburbs. In this country, native bird habitat disappears apace with the construction of human habitat. Compounding the situation, house sparrows and European starlings, which were introduced to North America in the 1800s, compete with native birds for what little habitat remains. Sadly, cavity-nesting birds are also threatened by our tendency as gardeners to trim every dead branch in the yard. By doing so, we rob the birds of natural nesting cavities and we deprive ourselves of their songs.

Putting up a birdhouse, also called a nesting box, is a simple way to replace lost habitats and to increase the variety of birds in your yard. Forty-eight species of birds are known to use birdhouses, including fly catchers, purple martins, wrens, nuthatches, swallows, and my favorite comedians, the black-capped chickadees. In addition to doing a good deed, providing homes for birds ensures that I have year-round allies in my battle with garden pests: "Look! A tasty tomato hornworm and some crunchy beetles to eat." Besides, I have found that birdhouses

Birdhouses located near a tree provide birds with a place to perch, such as when parent birds take turns feeding nestlings.

can be as beautiful as they are useful; so beautiful, in fact, that I succumb each time my local garden shop stocks a new one.

GOOD BIRDHOUSES HAVE DRAINAGE HOLES

Usable birdhouses can take myriad forms, from traditional nest boxes to hollowed-out gourds. Whatever design you choose should have specific characteristics, some of which are just what I want in my own house. I look for thick, insulating walls, a sloping roof to shed rain and snow, and a side- or front-opening access door (for late-winter cleaning). Unlike me, birds also appreciate drainage holes in the floor, ventilation holes near the roof, a rough or grooved interior to help the nestlings climb out of the box when they fledge, and a predator guard.

I stay away from birdhouses that have been treated or painted on the inside, as the chemicals may be harmful to nesting birds. I buy wooden birdhouses that are constructed with galvanized screws instead of glue or staples. A perch is not necessary for native cavity nesters.

Different birds require different size nest-box entrances. Eastern bluebirds, for example, need an opening that is precisely 1½ inches in diameter, while titmice want it only 1¼ inches across. Any birdhouse you buy should indicate the size of the opening and the varieties of birds that will use the box.

PLACE YOUR BIRDHOUSE HIGH ON A POLE OR POST

I hang birdhouses in late winter or early spring, when the birds arrive to search for nesting sites. Don't be discouraged if the birds don't use your box immediately; they

A sloping roof is just one of the characteristics that make a good birdhouse. Good drainage holes, predator guards, and thick, insulating walls are also important.

Birds that Commonly Use Nestboxes

SPECIES	ENTRANCE HOLE DIAMETER (INCHES)
Chickadee	1⅛
Titmouse	1¼
House wren	1¼
Bluebird	1½
White breasted nuthatch	1⅜
Tree swallow	1½
Hairy woodpeckers	1½
Northern flicker	2½
Screech owl	3 (10-30 ft. above ground)
Wood duck	4 (10-20 ft. above ground)

will find it in time. Attach the house to a pole or a post as high as you can reach for the annual cleaning. Position the opening away from the prevailing winds.

Squirrels, raccoons, and domestic cats are among nesting birds' most persistent predators. I have invested in predator guards to keep "my" birds safe from neighborhood cats. You can buy one of several styles of predator guards wherever birdhouses are sold.

Birds are choosy about where they live, and the location of your birdhouse will determine which species of birds come to visit. Tree swallows and bluebirds, for example, prefer sunny, open areas such as fields and large lawns. The nuthatches and chickadees in my yard love trees, while the wrens are perfectly content to remain close to buildings.

To attract woodland species, place the birdhouse within 15 feet of a shrub—preferably a fruiting shrub—where birds can perch as they come and go. This also ensures that if one parent is feeding the nestlings, the other parent has a place to wait. Wherever you place your birdhouse, make sure that you can see it easily, for watching your birds court, feed, and raise their young in your garden is very rewarding.

Birdhouses should be positioned high on a pole or post, with the opening away from the prevailing winds.

Birdhouses can be as beautiful as they are useful, ranging from simple to colorful to ornate.

The sloped roof of this birdhouse sheds rain, and nearby vegetation provides shade to keep interior temperatures cool.

VIRGINIA SMALL

is a *Fine Gardening* associate editor and nationally published poet. She accentuates the sculptural effects of many rock outcrops in her garden in northwestern Connecticut.

Garden
Benches–
beyond a
Place to Rest

Draw the eye toward a bench by placing it at the end of a path. This classic teak bench serves as both a focal point and a resting place.

S TRICTLY SPEAKING, a garden bench is simply a place to sit. Yet benches always perform double or triple duty in a garden, acting as focal points, design elements, or versatile structures. Benches often evoke feelings in me, such as stillness, whimsy, or expansiveness, even when viewed from a distance. I enjoy looking at well-placed benches almost as much as I like resting on them.

FORM FOLLOWS FUNCTION

The modernist architect Louis Sullivan influenced 20th-century attitudes with his adage that the form of something should follow its function. This line of thinking can lead to design solutions that are as beautiful as they are useful.

Before shopping for a bench, or building one, ponder what roles it might play. How long will you sit on it at any given time? How many people should it seat, and will it

Some benches merge into their surroundings. This stone one becomes part of a low wall in the garden.

Some benches are both whimsical and functional. Woolly thyme enhances the sensory experience of sitting on this stone bench.

A subtle background highlights a distinctive bench. The strong lines of this rustic seat are accentuated by a mass of deep-green foliage.

need companion furniture to inspire socializing? Will it nestle in a secret garden or be placed smack-dab in the middle of a patio on view from half the rooms in the house? How will weather affect its use and longevity?

With a bench intended for lounging, comfort should be the top priority. Something with a back support, arm rests, and the warm texture of wood might do the trick. I have a hankering for a swinging loveseat bench, like the one some friends placed to overlook a hillside. Of course, not all benches require such high standards of coziness. Seating made of filigreed wrought-iron, stone, or concrete may offer enough comfort for a brief respite.

STYLE CAN LEND SUBSTANCE

Whether rustic or ornate, the style of a garden bench invariably sets a mood. An appealing bench can invite a visitor to approach, to dream, to linger. The texture, shape, and color of a bench can work with plants and other structural elements to unify a garden space.

Benches work best when the mood they conjure suits the site. In Connecticut, garden writer Sydney Eddison's woodland garden is home to three rustic benches that offer views from different points around a pond. Two of the benches could be called minimalist furniture. Each is a long plank resting on two low tree stumps. The other is more intricate, with a slatted seat and backrest, as well as arm rests made of rounded limbs. All three blend harmoniously into the naturalistic setting, while more ornate or formal benches might seem out of place.

Another bench in a garden near Victoria, British Columbia, blends beautifully into its surroundings. Andrew Yeoman and Noel Richardson of Ravenhill Herb Farm built a stone bench that doubles as a planter for a lush bed of thyme. Rain kept me from actually sitting on that fragrant perch when I visited, but I brushed my hands through it before snapping

a few photos. I tacked one of those photographs on the wall above my desk because I love the way this bench seems both whimsical and primordial. It reminds me of the moss-covered rocks I encounter on woodland walks that inspire me to touch or even rest on them.

Sometimes a bench deserves to take center stage, such as when it's a weathered antique or a one-of-a-kind work of art. Many hand-carved, hand-painted, and stylized rustic benches are meant to be admired as well as used. Take advantage of their attention-getting power by using them as focal points or within vignettes with plants and other elements that accent the bench's color or texture.

SITE BENCHES FOR VIEWING— AND BEING VIEWED

Whether placed in an intimate, secret garden or overlooking a breathtaking vista, benches should face something that commands the

viewer's gaze. To make them visually appealing in their own right, benches need to be comfortably framed within a garden space. Too much space around a bench can make it look isolated or exposed, thus discouraging a visitor's approach. In contrast, placing a bench at the end of an allée or path will draw the eye and beckon a visitor forward.

Whether or not a bench has a backrest, its setting can provide a place to lean, as with a simple seat that wraps around a tree trunk. Vine-covered arbors, hedges, or multilayered plantings can enclose a bench and even make it feel like a throne.

While not every garden needs an arbor or a sundial, it seems that most planted spaces cry out for a bench of some sort. On a symbolic level, a bench invokes human participation. It calls out to us to enter a setting, to rest within it, and let its mysterious beauty unfold before our gaze.

Use a bench as the centerpiece of a vignette. An ornate, wrought-iron bench embellishes a richly textured planting.

LEE ANNE WHITE

is a consulting editor and former chief editor of *Fine Gardening*, a Master Gardener, and professional garden photographer.

Edging *Is* More

Than a Finishing Touch

This terra-cotta tile is a reproduction of the traditional English edger. It comes in several decorative patterns.

HAVE YOU, like me, ever had the urge to post a "No Trespassing" sign between your lawn and perennial border? Not for misdirected feet, but for unruly plants and spreading grasses that know no bounds? They're like overactive children who wiggle into places they're not wanted. So there we are—pulling stubborn clumps of Bermuda grass from otherwise well-manicured borders and scratching our heads over how to stop that little gaggle of gooseneck loosestrife from flocking into paths and lawns.

What we need is good edging. A bit of border control—on duty, around the clock, rain or shine. And with a little planning, edging can do double duty—adding visual structure to the garden or providing a convenient path for the wheel of a lawn mower to roll along.

Suitable for Small Spaces

Pricey? Yes. But how can you not fall for these antique and reproduction edgers? Try using them in a small space, such as a courtyard or patio garden, where attention to detail makes a big difference. This way, you can make a bigger impression with fewer edgers. And that's good, since bulk quantities of edgers are sometimes hard to find and the cost per tile is high. These are also areas that you can more easily tend by hand, so you can avoid the risk of damaging the tiles with power equipment.

Ornamental edgers are especially suited to formal gardens—perhaps partitioning off a petite knot garden—but they're also at home in informal settings. Some, like the rusted iron edger shown here, would be perfect for a quaint cottage garden. And if you have a small entry garden near your front door, they'd make a perfect welcoming statement setting off a mixed planting.

EDGING WITH A RICH HERITAGE

Although edgings have been used for centuries, their popularity peaked in the Victorian period. Scrounging around antique stores, I've assembled a modest collection of old edgers ranging from simple to fanciful. And many catalogs now offer reproduction clay, slate, cast-stone, wrought-iron, and galvanized edgers.

Most common are the traditional English tile or slate curbings with decorative patterns. Since they extend both below and above the ground, they not only look nice but also stop the subterranean spread of roots. Ornamental tiles add elegance to a formal garden, but either keep your garden small or be prepared to drop a few bucks—a 9-inch-wide tile costs $5 to $12, depending on the style and source.

Equally expensive are the Victorian wrought-iron, wire, and hoop edgings, or fencings. From fairly simple to unequivocally extravagant, these open-work edgers are strictly ornamental—only the stakes penetrate below ground. But who installs these beauties for practical purposes anyhow? They may divert some foot traffic, but their prime purpose is to ornament flower beds.

If you opt for ornamental edgers, it's best to use them around paths bordered by ground covers that don't need mowing. You can't mow cleanly next to them, and knocking delicate ornamental edgers with a lawn mower could easily damage or break them.

BRICK AND STONE ARE ATTRACTIVE, DURABLE, AND FUNCTIONAL

As much as I like the ornamental edgers, my property and wallet dictate something a little less elaborate and a little more affordable. As far as I'm concerned, brick and stone are the best all-around options for cost, durability, style, and usefulness.

When it comes to selecting brick or stone, the experts agree on one thing: Match the edging material to the style of your home. Formal architecture calls for brick or cut stone, such as cobbles. Random stone—like fieldstone, flagstone, or small boulders—is more appropriate for informal settings. Similarly, if you have a brick house, use brick edging. If your foundation is built from

Fencing is strictly decorative. It might deter a rabbit, but it's no match for spreading grasses, weeds, or perennials.

Set bricks at an angle for a saw-toothed effect. Here, the weathered bricks complement the colors of plants.

stone, use complementary stone for edgings. This way, you can make a visual connection between the landscape and the architecture.

In addition to style, select materials based on durability. Carl Romberg, construction manager of Atlanta's Habersham Gardens, notes that they often install cobbles between a driveway and lawn. "You need something heavy-duty here, and cobbles won't break if a car runs over them. Also, since the cobbles we use are roughly 4x4x8 inches, you can stand them on end with 4 inches above ground and 4 inches below ground, which makes the edging very sturdy."

For practicality, Romberg notes that brick makes the best mowing edge. "Ideally, bricks should be laid flush with the ground so that you can run the wheel of your mower along them. If your bricks extend above ground level, you'll have to come back with a weed trimmer to clean up the edges." Bricks and cobbles can be laid flat, on their sides, or on

end. And if mowing isn't an issue, you can lay bricks at an angle for a saw-toothed effect.

Unless your ground is solid and rarely suffers from heaving, it's best to set brick and stone edgers on a gravel or concrete base. Habersham Gardens usually installs brick and stone with mortar footings and joints. "This makes them sturdier," says Romberg. In Oakland, California, landscape architect Jeni Webber uses a 4-inch base of finely crushed, moistened, and tamped gravel, topped by a ¼- to ½-inch layer of builder's sand, with the joints filled with either sand or more crushed gravel. "If I just set bricks directly on the ground, they sink and settle," says Webber.

Random stones, such as small boulders, look more natural and help control the spread of plants if they are partially buried. Flagstones can be placed on end to create a barrier, and fieldstone can be stacked for raised beds. All random stones, when protruding aboveground, are ideal for keeping mulch in place in heavy rain.

Bricks, which are 8 inches long, usually cost less than 50 cents each. Cobbles, depending on size and style, run $1 to $2 apiece. Random stones may be gathered from your property or purchased from a stoneyard; prices depend on regional availability.

WOOD MAKES AN INFORMAL EDGING

In informal settings, wood is often used for edging. In fact, I just finished installing some 1x4-inch planks around my herb beds. First, I used the edging tool on my small tiller to trench the edges, and then I just set the planks, cut to length, in place. Corner pegs and a few nails secure and keep them straight. If the beds were curved, I could cut slits every inch or so in the wood to allow it to bend. In time, the wood will take on a nice weathered look.

Regional styles often dictate the use of wood. In some coastal Georgia developments, neighborhood covenants require beds and borders to be edged in pressure-treated, 1x4 lumber for uniformity. In California, redwood is often used as edging. In rustic settings, landscaping timbers or railroad ties may be appropriate, especially for raised beds.

An old-fashioned moat surrounds these tulips. Moats are an elegant, inexpensive approach to edging.

Random stones team up with polyvinyl strip edging to form a solid, yet attractive, barrier.

or plants threaten the border, you can spot them easily, grab your hoe, and stop the invasion before it becomes a nuisance.

Moats work best around clumping grasses like fescue and ryegrass. Spreading grasses like Bermuda grass and St. Augustine grass may keep you busy. At minimum, you'll need to patrol your moat with a shovel or hoe a couple of times over the growing season to maintain a crisp, weed-free border.

STRIP EDGINGS ARE INCONSPICUOUS, BUT EFFECTIVE

If you're looking for an edging that won't show, but don't feel up to patrolling a moat, you might opt for an underground barrier. The most common—polyvinyl strip edging—comes in rolls, usually 16 feet long and 5½ inches wide, with an upturned bottom edge and anchors to prevent heaving. The top edge is usually rounded and sits on the ground, so it isn't entirely invisible, but it is generally unobtrusive.

A porous version—with holes drilled through the edging every few inches—allows for drainage in difficult places. Another version doubles as an irrigation system, delivering water to your garden through tubing. And if you need a heavy-duty product, strip edging also comes in steel and aluminum, which is most often used by landscape contractors for commercial sites. To install strip edging, dig a trench, stretch out the edging, pound in several anchor pins, and then backfill with soil.

Another underground barrier is hard-plastic, pound-in edging, which is easier to install in loose soil—hard, rocky soils may require some prep work. These interlocking segments have jagged bottoms and are simply pounded into the ground. There's no trench

But no matter what kind of wood edging you install, keep in mind that all wood eventually rots in the ground. Pressure-treated lumber or creosote-treated ties will last longer than untreated wood, but some reports show that these chemicals can leach into the soil and plants—so avoid treated lumber if you are growing herbs, vegetables, or other edibles.

The cost of wood varies greatly, depending upon the type of wood, whether or not it has been treated, and current lumber pricing. However, if you're looking for a low-cost edging material and permanence isn't a factor, wood may be your best bet.

FOR NO-COST EDGING, DIG A TRENCH

The simplest (and cheapest) edging is little more than a mulched trench, or moat. Traditionally used to edge herbaceous borders in England, this V-shaped ditch is roughly 4 inches deep and wide. If your grass

to dig and no long length of unwieldy plastic to curl up on you like an uncooperative garden hose. Best of all, if you're working on a sloped site, you can stagger the height of the segments to go up or down hills like you would sections of fencing. The cost for strip and pound-in edging is roughly equivalent to brick or stone at 65 cents to $1.50 per running foot.

PLAN AHEAD FOR BEST RESULTS

If you intend to control the spread of grass and aggressive plants, you'll want your trench or edging material to be at least 4 to 6 inches deep. In loose, sandy soil, 8 inches is better. If you're dealing with something like bamboo, well, you'd better go even deeper—but that's another story. (There is, however, a new edging on the market that's made specifically for bamboo.)

Among gardeners, votes on "the best" edging are split. Atlanta garden designer Barbara Allen prefers a moat because she believes "the most important thing about edges is that they shouldn't show." Jeni Webber, however, likes edging materials in any kind of garden. "Distinct edges like brick and stone, even in an informal garden, create a sense of strength in the design, especially in winter."

As for me, I'm using a variety of edgings in the garden—moats, wood planks, and bricks. As for those antique Victorian edgers I've been collecting, well, they're great conversation pieces for the coffee table.

Brick borders aren't just for geometric gardens. Mortared brick lends a formal feel to this perennial border.

Credits

The articles compiled in this book appeared in the following issues of *Fine Gardening*:

p. 6: Fences, Walls, and Hedges Enclose a Garden (originally Fences, Walls, and Hedges Enclose a Garden with Character) by Lee Anne White, issue 65. Photos on pp. 6–7 (David Culp garden) and 10 (Elizabeth Sheldon garden) by Steve Silk, © The Taunton Press, Inc.; pp. 7 by Lee Anne White, © The Taunton Press, Inc.; p. 11 (Caprilands Herb Farm) © Lee Anne White; pp. 8 and 9 (Caroline Stevens garden) © J. Paul Moore.

p. 12: The Irresistible Appeal of Pickets by S. Andrew Schulman, issue 58. Photos on pp. 12, 14–15, and 16 © James P. Blair; p. 13 (author photo) by S. Andrew Schulman; p. 17 © Charles Mann; p. 18 © Allan Mandell; p. 19 © Kyle Morrison.

p. 20: Stacking a Dry Stone Wall by Andy Beasley, issue 54. Photos on pp. 20, 23, and 25 by Andy Beasley, © The Taunton Press, Inc.; p. 21 (author photo) by Peggy Beasley; pp. 22 (Hill Stead Museum garden, Farmington, CT) and 26–27 by Steve Silk, © The Taunton Press, Inc. Illustration by Gary Williamson.

p. 30: Paths Establish Cohesiveness and Style (originally Paths Establish Cohesiveness and Style in the Garden) by Gordon Hayward, issue 67. Photos on pp. 30 and 34 (Gordon Hayward garden, Putney, VT) and 32 (Pepsico garden, Purchase, NY) © Gordon Hayward; p. 31 (author photo) by Mary Hayward; pp. 33 (top) (Martha Berry garden, Rome, GA) and 35 (Atlanta History Center garden) © Lee Anne White; p. 33 (bottom) (Wesley Rouse garden, Southbury, CT) by Todd Meier, © The Taunton Press, Inc.

p. 36: Pathway Design Principles (originally Paths to Beauty) by Joe Parks, issue 31. Photos on p. 36 by Mark Kane, © The Taunton Press, Inc.; pp. 38, 39, 40, and 41 (right) by Chris Curless, © The Taunton Press, Inc.; p. 41 (left) by Susan Kahn, © The Taunton Press, Inc.

p. 42: Choosing Pavers for the Garden by Vincent Laurence, issue 61. Photos on p. 42 by Susan Kahn, © The Taunton Press, Inc.; p. 43 (author photo) by Anita Dafonte; pp. 44 and 49 (bottom) © Charles Mann; pp. 45, 46, 47, 48, and 49 (top) by Scott Phillips, © The Taunton Press, Inc.

p. 50: A Concrete Garden Path by S. Andrew Schulman, issue 70. Photos on pp. 50, 51 (author photo), 52, and 54 © S. Andrew Schulman.

p. 56: To Build a Brick Garden Path by Phyllis Gordon, issue 50. Photos on pp. 56, 60, 61, and 62 by Roger Foley, © The Taunton Press, Inc.; p. 57 (author photo) by J. R. Miller. Illustration by Gary Williamson.

p. 63: Make Your Own Stepping Stones (originally Stepping-Stones of Distinction) by Sally Roth, issue 48. Photos on pp. 63–67 by Boyd Hagen, © The Taunton Press, Inc.; p. 63 (author photo) by Daniel Knight; pp. 68 and 70 by staff.

p. 68: A Dry-Laid Paver Patio by Mary Anne Cassin, issue 20. Photos on pp. 68, 70 by staff, © The Taunton Press, Inc.; pp. 69 (author photo) and 73–75 © Kenneth E. Meyer. Illustration by Steve Buchanan.

p. 78: Structures to Grow On by Pam Baggett, issue 66. Photos on pp. 78, 83, and 84 by Lee Anne White, © The Taunton Press, Inc.; p. 80 © Ken Druse; pp. 81, 82, and 85 by Todd Meier, © The Taunton Press, Inc.

p. 86: Build a Rustic Garden Arbor by Frances Wenner, issue 69. Photos on pp. 86, 87 (author photo), and 91 © Bruce Wenner; pp. 88 and 90 © Frances Wenner. Illustration by Bob LaPointe.

p. 92: Lift Climbing Roses to New Heights (originally Structures Lift Climbing Roses to New Heights) by Lynn Hunt, issue 72. Photos on pp. 92 and 94–97 © Mike Shoup; p. 93 (author photo) © Lee Anne White.

p. 98: Handcrafting a Sturdy Arbor by Joe Taddia, issue 51. Photos on pp. 98, 101, 102, 103, and 104 by Steve Silk, © The Taunton Press, Inc.; p. 100 by Delilah Smittle, © The Taunton Press, Inc. Illustrations by Michael Gellatly.

p. 106: Build a Sapling Trellis by Sydney Eddison, issue 49. Photos on p. 107 by Steve Silk, © The Taunton Press, Inc.; pp. 106 and 109 (top) © Chris Curless; p. 109 (bottom) by Sydney Eddison. Illustrations by Michael Gellatly.

p. 111: Build a Copper Pipe Trellis (originally Build a Copper Trellis) by Donna Freeman, issue 53. Photos on p. 111 (bottom) © Allan Mandell; p. 111 (author photo) by Brandon Wentworth; pp. 114 and 115 by Steve Silk, © The Taunton Press, Inc. Illustration by Gary Williamson.

p. 118: Ornaments in the Garden by Eve Thyrum, issue 76. Photos by Lee Anne White, © The Taunton Press, Inc.

p. 126: Pool and Cascade by Des Kennedy, issue 28. Photos on pp. 126, 128, 130, and 133 by Paul Bailey; p. 127 (author photo) by Suzanne Hodges.

p. 134: Accentuate Art in the Garden by Virginia Small, issue 59. Photos on pp. 135, 137 (bottom), and 139 by Steve Silk, © The Taunton Press, Inc.; p. 134 © Derek St. Romaine; p. 136 © Andre Baranowski; p. 137 (top) © Keeyla Meadows; p. 138 © Lynne Harrison; p. 140 © Charles Mann; p. 141 © Allan Mandell.

p. 142: Sundials Lend a Sense of Time (originally Sundials Lend the Garden a Sense of Time and History) by Aurelia Scott, issue 68. Photos on pp. 143, 144, and 145 © Lee Anne White; p. 142 by Vincent Laurence, © The Taunton Press, Inc.

p. 146: A Fountain of Soothing Sounds by Steve Silk, issue 62. Photos on pp. 146 and 147 by Steve Silk, © The Taunton Press, Inc.; pp. 149 and 150 by Virginia Small, © The Taunton Press, Inc. Illustration by Gary Williamson.

p. 151: Birdhouses Attract Wildlife (originally Where You Position Your Birdhouse Determines Which Species of Birds Come to Visit) by Aurelia Scott, issue 71. Photos on pp. 151, 152, and 155 © Lee Anne White; pp. 153 and 154 by Todd Meier, © The Taunton Press, Inc.

p. 156: Garden Benches—Beyond a Place to Rest (originally A Garden Bench is More than Just a Place to Rest) by Virginia Small, issue 69. Photos on p. 156 © Lee Anne White; pp. 157 and 159 by Steve Silk, © The Taunton Press, Inc.; p. 158 (top right, top left) by Virginia Small, © The Taunton Press, Inc.; p. 158 (bottom) © J. Paul Moore.

p. 160: Edging Is More than a Finishing Touch by Lee Anne White, issue 63. Photos by Lee Anne White, © The Taunton Press, Inc.

Front matter photo credits

p. ii: Steve Silk, © The Taunton Press, Inc.
p. iii: © Derek St. Romaine.
p. vi: (left) © James P. Blair.
p. vi: (right) Chris Curless, © The Taunton Press, Inc.
p. vii: (left): Mike Shoup.
pp. vii (top right), 2: Lee Anne White, © The Taunton Press, Inc.
p. vii (bottom right): © Allan Mandell.

Section openers photo credits

p. 4: Steve Silk, © The Taunton Press, Inc.
p. 5: © Allan Mandell.
p. 28: Boyd Hagen, © The Taunton Press, Inc.
p. 29: Chris Curless, © The Taunton Press, Inc.
pp. 76 and 77: © Mike Shoup.
p. 116: Steve Silk, © The Taunton Press, Inc.
p. 117: Lee Anne White, © The Taunton Press, Inc.

Index